Preparing
New
Teachers

This series is dedicated in loving memory
to my parents, Daisy Lea and Weldon F. Appelt.
Through their love and devotion for me, I learned to
believe in myself and what I might be able to achieve in life.

Preparing
New
Teachers

Operating
Successful
Field
Experience
Programs

Editor
Gloria Appelt Slick

CORWIN PRESS, INC.
A Sage Publications Company
Thousand Oaks, California

For information address:

Corwin Press, Inc.
A Sage Publications Company
2455 Teller Road
Thousand Oaks, California 91320

SAGE Publications Ltd.
6 Bonhill Street
London EC2A 4PU
United Kingdom

SAGE Publications India Pvt. Ltd.
M-32 Market
Greater Kailash I
New Delhi 110 048 India

Printed in the United States of America

Library of Congress Cataloging-in-Publication Data

Preparing new teachers: operating successful field experience
  programs / edited by Gloria Appelt Slick.
      p. cm.
  Includes bibliographical references and index.
  ISBN 0-8039-6208-8 (alk. paper). — ISBN 0-8039-6209-6 (pbk.:
alk. paper)
  1. Student teaching—United States—Planning. 2. Student
teachers—Supervision of—United States.   I. Slick, Gloria Appelt.
LB2157.U5P74   1995
370'.7'330973—dc20   95-6658

This book is printed on acid-free paper.

95 96 97 98 99 10 9 8 7 6 5 4 3 2 1

Corwin Project Editor: Susan McElroy

Contents

Foreword

Student teaching has long been considered the capstone of the teacher education program, and early field experiences have recently become a vital part of preparing teachers. Most teacher educators believe that field experiences should be integrated into the preparation of future teachers.

Because of this emphasis on field experiences, the position of director of field experiences has become even more important in teacher education. Where can field directors receive the information necessary to carry out the many and varied duties of the position? They tend to ask other field directors' advice. One of the most popular opportunities for field directors to share ideas is through membership in the National Field Directors' Forum, an affiliate with the Association of Teacher Educators.

The tenure of a field director is relatively short. The average tenure is between 3 and 5 years. Because of the turnover of field directors, there always seem to be new field directors literally craving information that will help them perform their duties.

Field directors recognize the need for some books that contain the information that both experienced and new field directors could use as a reference. A series of four books dealing with all aspects of field experiences, edited by Dr. Gloria Appelt Slick, fulfills the need. Directors around the nation welcome this series and I am proud to endorse this effort.

ELDEN R. BARRETT, PH.D.
FORMER PRESIDENT, NATIONAL FIELD DIRECTORS' FORUM

Foreword

Dear Educator:

As you read the material presented in this four-book series dealing with field experiences in teacher preparation programs, I hope you will bear in mind that this unique project is being brought to you from an institution whose history is rich in and founded upon teacher education. It has been through the leadership and dedication of such educators as Dr. Gloria Appelt Slick, editor of this series, that The University of Southern Mississippi, which was founded as Mississippi's normal school in 1910, continues to take a leadership role in the professional training of teachers.

I am proud to share with you this most recent endeavor of Dr. Slick, which focuses on the significance of field experiences in teacher preparation. Recent research by the Holmes Group, John Goodlad, and such accrediting agencies as the National Council for the Accreditation of Teacher Education has underscored the importance of the field experiences component of teacher education programs. This series of four books provides a review of state-of-the-art programs and practices in field experiences. The contributing authors represent prestigious teacher preparation programs from around the country. The information presented herein is solidly grounded in both research and practice. One of the main purposes of the four books is to provide practical guidelines for application of effective programs and practices in field experiences.

This is not the first time Dr. Slick has produced a national project that emphasizes field experiences. In 1993, through a national teleconference under the auspices of the Satellite Educational Resources Consortium, four interactive distance learning programs were broadcast to more than 200 sites nationally for the purpose of assisting student teachers, during their student teaching experiences, with their transition from university students to classroom teachers. From that series and the research involved to produce it evolved the current books, whose purpose reaches beyond student teachers and encompasses all persons, processes, and institutions affected by the field experiences component of teacher education. In both cases, Dr. Slick's overall goal has been to provide assistance and direction for all those involved in field experiences so that students of teacher education will be better prepared to meet the challenges of teaching the children of today and tomorrow.

Teacher education will always remain a major focus at The University of Southern Mississippi. We are committed to excellence in our teacher preparation programs and strive to develop the best of each of our students' abilities and expertise as future teachers. It is through such efforts as Dr. Slick's that we strive to meet that commitment.

Best wishes,

AUBREY K. LUCAS
PRESIDENT, THE UNIVERSITY OF SOUTHERN MISSISSIPPI

Preface

As a result of the Holmes Report, "A Nation at Risk," and other research, the wheels have been set in motion for a reflective and systemic change in the education profession. Both public schools and institutions of higher learning have had the national public spotlight on the quality of their educational outcomes and teacher preparation programs respectively. Institutions of higher learning have adjusted their content and pedagogical requirements in their teacher education programs to try to meet the challenges of children who are products of the information age. Public schools have updated curricular offerings and made concerted efforts to tackle the innumerable problems relative to providing students and faculties with safe environments in which to teach and learn. Research by such educational leaders as Goodlad, Berliner, and Boyer emphasizes that the teachers of the future will need to participate early and continuously during their teacher preparation programs in the public school arena where they will eventually be employed. Nationwide, school districts and universities are forming collaborations that not only provide insight into the culture of the teaching profession for the novice teacher but also offer opportunities for veteran teachers to retool their skills as well as share their expertise with upcoming generations of new teachers. In essence, this bridge between the universities and the public schools, whether in the form of a professional development school, or a lab school, or local public school campus, provides the pathway from student to teacher.

The program planning and management required to provide students in teacher preparation programs the opportunity to successfully cross the bridge from student to teacher are very complex. The bulk of the responsibility for providing students this successful crossing relies upon the collaborative success of teacher preparation programs and offices of educational field experiences. The director of the field experiences programs plays a principal role in managing the various persons and systems involved in the transitional passage of students to beginning teachers. It has been well documented by research that field experiences are the pivotal turning points in students' preparation for becoming teachers. During those experiences theory meets practice, and students discover whether they can teach—or even want to teach. To date, for all persons and entities involved in this process, there is very little, if any, material available to assist in providing the best possible experiences for students aspiring to become exemplary teachers. The goal of this series of books is to provide field directors the information and practical guidance necessary to design and implement a successful field experience program that will provide individuals in teacher preparation programs a smooth transition from student to teacher.

Because the focus of these books is to provide information and practical guidance to all persons involved with field experiences in teacher preparation programs, it became a foregone conclusion that those persons contributing to this book should either be currently affiliated or have been recently affiliated with field experience programs. Most of the authors have actually been field experience directors, with the exception of those in specialty areas such as law and public school administration. In order for the book to be representative of a national view of the issues related to field experiences, much time and effort went into selecting persons representing a variety of types of institutions as well as geographic locations around the country. Attention has been given to the size of the teacher preparation programs offered at the various institutions that are represented in the books, with the intent to provide as many relevant views about field experience programs as possible in order to benefit cohorts everywhere. Institutions represented from the southeast include the states of

Alabama, Louisiana, Mississippi, Florida, and North Carolina; the northeast includes the states of New Jersey, New York, Pennsylvania, and Delaware; the midwestern states include Ohio, Kentucky, Illinois, Michigan, Iowa, Indiana, and Minnesota; the central states include Oklahoma and Texas; and the western states include Colorado, Arizona, Utah, and California.

Organization of the Books

To provide information and practical guidance for all the issues related to field experience programs, there are four books, each with a specific purpose. Book I, *The Field Experience: Creating Successful Programs for New Teachers*, provides information about the development and organization of field experience programs. It presents state-of-the-art field experience programs and explains what kinds of experiences should be provided to students. Other issues in Book I include the dilemma of the department chair who must provide a program that creates a balance between theory and practica, the dean's perspective of the significance of field experiences in teacher training, and the evaluation processes needed for field experiences programs. Book II, *Preparing New Teachers: Operating Successful Field Experience Programs*, presents practical ideas concerning the operation and function of the field experiences office and takes into account state department requirements relative to certification that also have an impact on field experience programs. Such issues as placement procedures as well as displacement procedures and the legal ramifications of both are discussed. The multifaceted responsibilities of the field director are presented, which brings to light the public relations that the director must handle, not only with the public schools, but also across the various colleges and departments at a university/college. In addition, the purposes of field experiences handbooks are explained. Book III, *Making the Difference for Teachers: The Field Experience in Actual Practice*, addresses the needs and responsibilities of the persons involved in a typical field experience paradigm— the university student, public school personnel, and university personnel. Key issues like effective communication and classroom management skills, effective mentoring, and adequate training of cooperating teachers are presented. Field experiences are explained from the student teacher's perspective, and the process of the student's assimilation of the culture of teaching is addressed. A major issue of concern is the preparation of cooperating teachers for the responsibility of supervising students. This is also dealt with in Book III. In addition, suggestions are made for ways to express appreciation to those who work so diligently supervising student teachers and other practicum students. Each of these issues has an impact on the university students' success during field experiences, and each topic is delivered in practical and applicable terms. Book IV, *Emerging Trends in Teacher Preparation: The Future of Field Experiences*, addresses areas of special interest affecting field experiences: (a) the promotion of reflective practices throughout all field experiences in teacher preparation programs; (b) the multicultural classroom environments education students will have to face; (c) the effective utilization of technology in field experience programs; (d) the awareness of legal ramifications of policies, or the lack of them, in field experience programs; (e) the development of leadership potential in preservice teachers; (f) the support for the first year on the job; and (g) the special opportunities for student teaching field experiences abroad. A new look at the psychology of supervision is also presented, along with a view of how the past can help us shape the future in field experiences. At the end of each book, there is a chapter titled "Bits and Pieces" that presents other issues that are critical to the overall success of field experience programs. Key points mentioned in each book are synthesized and analyzed. The information is presented in a somewhat encapsulated view, along with additional points that may need mentioning.

The composite focus of all four books in the series is to provide the information and operational examples to assist others in offering strong, challenging, and viable field experience programs throughout the country. The reader will find that each topic addressed in all the books will place an emphasis on the practical application of the ideas and information presented. The series of books will provide readers not only with "food for thought" but also "food for action."

Acknowledgments

A massive project like this is only possible because of many wonderful people contributing their expertise, time, and energy to making it happen. From all over the country friends and colleagues worked diligently to contribute their special pieces to the books. My sincere appreciation to my authors who patiently worked with me to complete this series.

Thanks also go to my office staff, Tina Holmes and Diane Ross, and to my university supervisors, Drs. Donna Garvey, Tammie Brown, Betsy Ward, and Ed Lundin, who kept the office running smoothly while I labored over "the books," as they came to be known in the office. Our office teamwork and philosophy of operation paid off during this project. Thanks go to my graduate assistants, Leslie Peebles and Amy Palughi, whose hard work during the initial stages of this project launched us with a good beginning. Most especially thanks go to Mrs. Lauree Mills Mooney, whose organizational and computer skills made it possible for the project to be pulled together in a timely manner. Mrs. Mooney's resourcefulness in overcoming obstacles and dedication toward completing the project were invaluable. In the final stages of proofing and indexing all the books, I want to thank Ms. Holly Henderson for her timely and critical assistance.

Thanks to special friends who encouraged me throughout the project: Dr. Margaret Smith, Dr. Kenneth Burrett, Dr. Chuck Jaquith, and Dr. Sandra Gupton.

The timely production and final completion of all four books could not have occurred without the kind and caring encouragement and guidance of the Corwin Press staff. My sincere thanks go to Alice Foster, Marlene Head, Wendy Appleby, Susan McElroy, and Lin Schonberger for their understanding and patience throughout this project.

A special thanks to my husband, Sam Slick, for his constant encouragement and support. Also, special thanks to my children, Andrew and Samantha, who patiently tiptoed around the house so Mom could think and compose in order to finish "the books."

About the Contributors

Genevieve Brown, currently a professor and chair of Educational Leadership and Counseling at Sam Houston State University, formerly served as coordinator of secondary education and supervisor of students teachers at SHSU. Previously, she was a middle and high school teacher and served in various administrative roles in public schools, including 10 years as assistant superintendent for curriculum and instruction. A frequent presenter at state and national conferences and author of several articles on teacher effectiveness, curriculum and instruction, and leadership, she was recently named the Outstanding Instructional Leader in Texas and Outstanding Woman Educator in the state.

Kenneth Burrett is a professor in the school of education at Duquesne University and an associate in the center for character education, civic responsibility, and teaching. He also serves as a charter faculty member for Duquesne University's Interdisciplinary Doctoral Program for Education Leaders. A former elementary and secondary teacher and high school department chair, he has served as director of student teaching and associate dean at Duquesne. He received his bachelor of arts and master of science degrees from Canisius College and his Ed.D. from the State University of New York at Buffalo. He is active in Phi Delta Kappa, the Pennsylvania Association of Colleges and Teacher Educators (PAC-TE), and the Association for Teacher Educators (ATE). He was named Teacher Educator of the Year in 1989 by the Pennsylvania Unit of ATE. He serves on the board of Conservation Consultants, a nonprofit environmental organization; is past president of Western Pennsylvania Council for the Social Sciences; and serves on the board of PAC-TE and various committees of ATE. He has also secured numerous grants for inservicing veteran science teachers and encouraging career change individuals to enter teaching. This past year he coauthored a book chapter and *Phi Delta Kappa Fastback*, both concerned with integrated character education. He has also delivered numerous papers in the area of leadership theory and program design.

Jan Cross coordinates the teacher preparation programs at California State University, Sacramento. Her experience includes secondary public school teaching; doctoral study at Wisconsin, Stanford, and Pitt, where she earned a Ph.D. in English-Education; and 25 years of university teaching and supervising of student teachers at California State University, Sacramento. In a typical recent semester, California State University, Sacramento placed hundreds of student teachers in 162 Sacramento area schools with 645 cooperating teachers.

Beverly J. Irby received her Ed.D. in curriculum and instruction from the University of Mississippi. Over the past 18 years she has been an elementary and middle school teacher, school psychologist, educational diagnostician, special education director, elementary school principal, director of field experiences, assistant superintendent, and interim superintendent of schools. She is a researcher of women's leadership issues, as well as of science and gifted education. She is listed in the *International Who's Who of Women* and has received the Texas Council of Women School Executives' Outstanding Educator Award. She is the co-editor of a book on women in leadership and coauthor of two books on teen pregnancy and parenting.

Charles E. Jaquith has 22 years' experience as a middle school teacher and principal, including 6 years as a laboratory school principal. In this position he coordinated pre-student teaching and student teaching field activities. For 18 years he supervised student teachers for Central Michigan University. During the past 5 years he has directed their field experience programs and has implemented two additional levels of field-based experiences. Jaquith has presented at professional conventions and is past president of the National Field Directors' Forum.

Dale L. Lange, formerly the associate dean for academic affairs, is currently a professor of educational policy and administration in the College of Education at the University of Minnesota. His areas of interest are second language education, teacher development, professional development schools, and policy matters relating to teacher licensure. He is currently president of the Minnesota Association of Colleges for Teacher Education.

Joy Millar began her association with Northern Arizona University in 1993, as a supervisor of 20 student teachers in the Verde Valley area of northern Arizona. In August of 1993 she was hired for her current position of program coordinator. Her career in education spans a 27-year period in Texas as a secondary teacher, where she taught for Hallettsville I.S.D., Yoakum I.S.D., and Cypress Fairbanks I.S.D. in Houston, Texas.

Martha M. Mobley received her education at State University of New York College at Oneonta, Adelphi University, and New York University, completing her Ph.D. in 1988. The topic of her dissertation, which combines her professional educational interest with her personal community commitment, was an examination of the policies, procedures, and practices of public schools and the delivery of programs to adolescent pregnant and parenting students. She has observed and participated in the formal education system as a classroom teacher, a building and central office administrator, and a university professor. As a specialist with Cornell Cooperative Extension she designed and delivered programs to day-care providers, personnel of health and social service agencies, and senior citizens. One project, Red Wagon: A Training Program for Young Teens and Family Day Care Providers, was replicated in such states as Michigan, Kansas, and Wyoming. She currently directs the Teaching Performance Center at Kean College of New

Jersey, a field experience office through which more than 2,000 students are placed each year. In this work she is most interested in developing cluster placements for student teachers, so that collaborative efforts between public schools and the college can be engendered, and learning communities for preservice and in-service educators can be modeled.

Gloria Appelt Slick, a native of Houston, Texas, completed her doctoral work at the University of Houston in 1979. Her professional career in public school education has included classroom teaching, supervision, the principalship, and assistant superintendency for curriculum. In her current position as a faculty member of the Department of Curriculum and Instruction and as Director of Educational Field Experiences at The University of Southern Mississippi in Hattiesburg, Mississippi, her past public school experiences have provided her with significant insight into the circumstances and needs of public schools for well-trained beginning teachers. During her tenure as Director of Field Experiences, Dr. Slick has produced, in conjunction with Mississippi Educational Television, the first interactive distance learning program to deal with the subject of field experiences, titled "From Student to Teacher." These four programs were aired nationally in March 1993 and received the Mississippi Public Education Forum Award for Excellence that same year. Dr. Slick is currently president of the National Field Directors' Forum, affiliated with the Association of Teacher Educators. She also serves on the editorial board of *The Teacher Educator*. Her current research interests center on teacher preparation programs and, in particular, the interface of field experiences with those programs. Technological integration into the field experience programs and field experiences abroad are also high on her list of research and programmatic implementation.

Edward M. Vertuno earned a B.A. in English, in 1954, from St. Mary's College, Winona, Minnesota; an M.A. in English, in 1955, from Northwestern University; and an Ed.D. in educational administration, in 1971, from the University of Illinois. His professional experience includes 10 years as a secondary classroom teacher, 4 years as a high school principal, 18 years as director of a K-12 university laboratory school, and 3 years as a supervisor of student teachers. He is currently director of student teaching for the College of Education at Florida State University.

Introduction

GLORIA APPELT SLICK

The effective functioning of a successful field experience program and the office personnel who manage it is unbelievably complex. The program and the people who operate it serve so many and such a variety of publics it becomes almost impossible to imagine all the many responsibilities and tasks to be accomplished. The chapters found in *Preparing New Teachers: Operating Successful Field Experience Programs* address the operational aspects of a successfully functioning field experience program and office. The processes, components, and people making successful field experiences occur in teacher education programs are described and explained in relationship to their function to the overall program. The who, what, and how of this vitally important and integral part of teacher preparation programs are presented in order to provide descriptive applications of the necessary, viable means for creating successfully functioning programs. How do programs operate, how are schedules set, and how does effective communication take place among all the various groups/ publics involved? How are program decisions made, and how are program changes made and then implemented? Who guides the program, and who is responsible for the success of the program?

Who advises and makes program changes? Who composes the typical office staff? What are the qualifications of the program director, university supervisors, and office staff? What is the annual schedule of events in a field experience program, and who is responsible for setting the schedule? What content and/or topics of instruction are included in the program? What type of office management strategies best fit the field experience office? All of these questions and many more are relative to both the operation of a field experience program and the office making it possible.

In any organization the type of management of the services and products provided by the organization for public use can and usually does make or break the success of that organization. By the same token, the manner by which the people in an organization are led and managed can also be the definitive factor that determines the success of that organization. Services and effective office management become the focal points of a field experience program and office.

The field experience office is an organization whose main function is one of service to a variety of publics that share the common bond of being engaged in some aspect of teacher preparation. The means by which these various groups arrive at the same conclusion is not always the same. Perceptions differ greatly among these groups as to the best manner in which to prepare students to become effective teachers. However, an effective interface of the various groups engaged in teacher education is necessary if successful field experiences are to occur in all those programs. These varying perspectives of teacher education include (a) teacher preparation programs outside the college of education whose focus is on content acquisition and the development of a solid knowledge base with very little pedagogical preparation or field experiences; (b) colleges of education, which include subject matter concentrations, but whose emphasis is typically on the pedagogical and field experiences connections among them; (c) public schools whose focus is on the performance proficiency of a potential teacher and on providing experiences that meet their current needs in the workplace (note that the concern in public schools, many times out of necessity, is not so much on new and innovative ways of teaching as it is on meeting state curricular requirements as well as making certain their pupils obtain high scores on standardized tests); (d) state certification agencies' view of teacher preparation from the perspective of criteria being met for certification; and (e) the general public's wanting good teachers and good schools, but not seeming to understand the process or wanting to participate in the process to make it happen, nor wanting to be taxed at a higher rate to fund more equitable efforts for children's education. Sitting squarely in the middle of all these groups is the field experience office, which must serve, please, and appease all of these groups in order for preservice teachers to experience the necessary and, hopefully, the kind of enrichment experiences that will allow them to become the best possible teachers they can be. Teachers are needed who can meet the challenges ahead in the teaching profession and can best serve the diversified needs of children in the future.

The keys to the bridge that the field experience office must build among all these groups are communication and collaboration. Preservice teacher education is a collaborative effort by schools and universities to achieve a complex common goal: effective beginning teachers (Schumacher, Rommel-Esham, & Bauer, 1987, p. 3). Collaboration implies a mutual interdependence, collegial in nature, for producing a comprehensive teacher preparation program (Lanier, 1983; Lieberman, 1986; Maeroff, 1983; Maloy, 1985). Collaboration suggests that each institution is willing to make internal institutional changes to attain the common goal of teacher effectiveness (Schumacher et al., 1987, p. 3). The degree to which each institution and its component parts is willing to make changes directed at a common goal is one of the most significant keys to a successful field experience program. The very difficult job of assisting all interested parties' ability to focus on a common goal befalls the field director and all persons working within the field experience office. Therefore, it is of utmost importance that the vision of the field director and those working in the field experience office be a common one. If the core office's vision is not unified, it will be very difficult for a common vision for the entire program to be achieved. A set of common generic objectives for preservice teachers determined by school and university teacher educators appears essential to plan, develop, and evaluate an internally consistent teacher education program (Darling-Hammond, Wise, & Pease, 1985).

References

Darling-Hammond, L., Wise, A. I., & Pease, S. R. (1985). Teacher evaluation in the organizational context: A review of the literature. *Review of Educational Research, 53*(3), 285-328.

Lanier, J. E. (1983). Tensions in teaching teachers the skills of pedagogy. In G. Griffin (Ed.), *Staff development. 82nd yearbook for the national society for the study of education. Part II.* Chicago: University of Chicago Press.

Lieberman, A. (1986). Collaborative research: Working with, not working on. . . . *Educational Leadership, 43*(5), 28-32.

Maeroff, G. I. (1983). *School and college.* Princeton, NJ: Princeton University Press.

Maloy, R. (1985). The multiple realities of school-university collaboration. *The Educational Forum, 49*(3), 341-350.

Schumacher, S., Rommel-Esham, K., & Bauer, D. (1987, April). *Professional knowledge objectives for preservice teachers as determined by school and university teacher educators.* Paper presented at the AERA Annual Meeting, Washington, DC.

Qualifications and Responsibilities of the Field Experience Director

GLORIA APPELT SLICK

Responsibilities of the Field Director

Warning! If you cannot manage several major issues and groups of people simultaneously, with a smile and a casual attitude, this job is not for you. The field director must wear a variety of hats in a variety of settings. He or she must be a master at getting along with people in innumerable institutional and informal settings. Answerable to many publics, this person must have a broad conceptual understanding of how numerous entities work together in concert toward an ultimate goal—the professional training of preservice teachers. With so much recent research placing emphasis on the significance of field experiences in teacher training, field experiences are no longer looked upon as principally the student teaching experience. Now field directors find themselves orchestrating and managing a continuum of field experiences throughout teacher preparation programs. This is an exciting challenge and one that requires a person who has a certain type of personality and love for the profession in order for that person to enjoy his or her responsibilities.

Publics Served

Dealing with so many publics basically necessitates the utilization of a participatory management style if the director is to represent the concerns and wishes of those he or she serves. At the university level the field director often negotiates program decisions and operation with executive administrators, including the president, academic vice president, fiscal management director, registrar, vice president for student affairs, vice president for research, and university legal counsel. Other managers with whom a field director often works are the director of academic computing, the director of food services, the director of campus security, the director of library media services, the director of the office of research and sponsored programs, the director of a campus print shop, and the bookstore director. Planning for and serving all the colleges on campus necessitates the field director's working with the deans of all the respective colleges in which teacher preparation programs are housed, the department chairs of departments offering teaching certification, and the various faculties of those departments that teach methods classes and/or supervise practicum students.

Most state departments have specific guidelines for the amount of time and the description of the circumstances under which student teaching should occur. Consequently, there is constant communication between the field experience office and the state department. In particular, the office of field experience works closely with the certification office at the state department.

Still another group of people the field director serves and works with are the university students and their families, particularly when placements for student teaching are being made. In the public schools, field directors are in constant contact with central office administrators—superintendents, assistant superintendents, fiscal managers, supervisors of curriculum—as well as with principals and teachers at individual school buildings.

Most field directors belong to and utilize networks with cohorts at both the state and national levels as well. These opportunities are available through professional organizations.

Leadership Style of Field Directors

Because field directors have to deal with so many different publics, their leadership style should be one of transformational leadership. This type of leader motivates others by transforming their self-interest into the goals of the organization. In the organization of tomorrow, leading is defined as the process of influencing others to achieve mutually agreed-upon purposes for the organization (Patterson, 1993, p. 3). This type of leadership has evolved from the educational reform movements, which have given birth to systemic change. Basically, advocates of systemic change hypothesize that no one component of an organization can change without having an impact on the whole organization. Consequently, if changes are to be made, then the whole system must be involved in the change process. According to Slick and Gupton:

> Systemic reform, therefore, takes into consideration the interrelatedness of all the components which function together in the education system, and realizes that as one component changes, so must the others in order to maintain the integrity, continuity and consistency of the entire system. To accomplish this goal, all players in the system must be considered as viable, potential and on-going contributors to the change process. (Slick & Gupton, 1993, p. 2)

Because field experience programs have an impact on so many publics, it stands to reason that those affected by the change should have a voice in the changes under consideration. Systemic change also requires the organization's component parts to have a common vision that remains paramount so that divisive distractions will not deter the ultimate goal of the organization. Therefore, it is critical that the director realize that the basic purpose of the field experience office is to serve all the various publics and guide and direct them toward an agreed-upon goal. The field director who can successfully incorporate the transformational leadership style will have the entire organization of numerous publics working toward the common goal of producing the best quality beginning teachers possible.

Communication Requirements

Because field experiences programs encompass so many facets of both a university and public school life, the director communicates and negotiates with many "chiefs" who have ultimate decision-making power for their respective programs. This makes it almost impossible for a field director to make a unilateral decision and necessitates collaborative decision making among all publics involved. Most of the director's time, however, is spent negotiating with four major publics: (a) colleges within the university, their deans, chairs, and faculty who deal with teacher education; (b) public schools, their central office administrators, principals, and teachers; (c) the state department of education; and (d) the university students. Critical to the success of any director are communication skills, both written and oral. One cannot be a field director and shirk the crowd; he or she is in the midst of the crowd. Open and honest communication is critical. When conversing on the phone or in person, polite and professional dialogue is always appropriate. State clearly your purpose for calling and then listen carefully to the responses given. Avoid assumptions concerning information related to the conversation and carefully attend to the person's words and tone of voice. Many misunderstandings can be avoided if careful listening and responsive comments address the speaker's remarks. Field directors must, therefore, have effective people skills that support their ability to communicate well.

Much of what a field director communicates will be in the form of written correspondence. This may be a memo, a business letter, a personal note, a friendly letter, specific forms to be completed, and/or something as formal and all-encompassing as the field experience handbook. All forms of written correspondence must be carefully monitored, professionally done, spell checked, grammar checked, and form checked so that the resultant correspondence presents the office of field experience, and ultimately the university, in the best light possible. Many times it is the written word that makes or breaks the success of a field experience program, because written documents may be the only form of communication accessible to some of the publics that the field experience office serves. The director must think carefully about the need for and purpose of a written document. Some documents are very formal, such as the legal contracts between school districts and universities outlining their agreed-upon arrangement for field placements. Others may be an expression of appreciation for a job well done and may even be handwritten.

There is a definite need for a paper trail to document communication and business transactions. The state department requires certain records to be kept on file that verify students' completion of program requirements for certification. Accurate accounting of each student's placement process is critical for office management integrity as well as positive relations with the public schools and other colleges on the campus. Paper documentation provides a hard copy history of the business occurring under the guidance of the field director. It is of utmost importance to have any computerized database of students, office forms, and office policies saved on both the hard drive and a backup disk along with hard copies.

Future communication possibilities that would be beneficial in field experience programs include E-mail, the Internet, and compressed video options. Video cameras and playback units should be standard equipment that can be utilized to record exemplary teaching by students as well as public school teachers.

Ultimately, it is important to note that both oral and written communication are vitally important to the success of a field experience program. It is the director of the program who is responsible for generating and disseminating both mediums of communication. Consequently, successful directors will be effective communicators.

Field Director
Personality and Qualifications

Personality

Who is this person called the field director? What kind of personality and qualifications must he or she possess? When you meet these people there are some unique characteristics that consistently surface. They are kind, caring people who believe that being a teacher educator is an important responsibility. They believe that their efforts to produce quality teachers can make a difference for children. They are among the most hard working and most flexible people you will meet in the profession. Their lives are constantly affected by the varying needs of the publics they serve. They like people; they like helping people. They are capable of seeing the good in everyone and they are fiercely dedicated to the principles of quality education for all. They are well grounded on one side in theory and research, and on the other in the real-world application of those theories and research. They like that dual role because it is very much like being a part of the best of both the world of academia and the world of practice. They learn to become sensitive to the politics of the systems in which they work. They want their voice to be heard above the deafening roar and political clamoring for a "piece of the pie." They want their piece because they believe that what they are doing is important for children.

Field directors typically have had successful careers in public education as well as higher education. That is why they feel comfortable in both arenas. They are energetic, open-minded risk takers who constantly search for and create the most innovative and proven programs for successful field experiences in teacher preparation. They are typically bright people capable of visionary decision making. They lead by generating ideas that motivate others in the system to action. They possess sophisticated organizational skills that allow them to assess both day-to-day operational needs and broad-based, long-term needs. To create state-of-the-art programs, they engage in research and writing endeavors that keep them abreast of the latest in teacher preparation and public school education.

Professional Qualifications

To be effective as a field director, a person must have achieved a certain level of professional status. It is important that two of the major publics being served, the university and the public schools, view this person as competent in their respective arenas. Consequently, obtaining faculty rank at the university provides the usual collegial relationship that all other faculty possess. Being a member of a specific department allows for a research and teaching connection with other professional colleagues. Obtaining university faculty status generally requires that the person has completed a Ph.D. or Ed.D. degree. Membership in a department and terminal degree status can go a long way toward assisting the director with all the necessary university business and negotiations for the field experience programs.

To achieve a level of respect and acceptance among public school personnel, the field director must have teaching experience, and preferably administrative or supervisory experience, in the public school setting. Such a person would have a sensitivity to the needs and limitations of the public schools. In dealing with public schools, a director must be aware that the university's program and all the people associated with it are guests in the public school system, and that with or without the university's presence, the public schools already have a busy and full agenda of business. Therefore, it is an absolute necessity that there is a mutually agreeable operational plan for university personnel and students to exist and function within the framework of an already existing, complex public school system.

The active, progressive director networks professionally. At the state and national levels, directors gather in special interest groups to share experiences and research conclusions. The National Field Directors' Forum, a special interest group affiliated with the Association of Teacher Educators, is one of the strongest of these groups.

Additional Responsibilities of the Field Director

Research and Program Evaluation

A great deal of emphasis has already been placed on the liaison role that a field director must play in order to maintain good public relations with all the various publics being served. Numerous other responsibilities consume a field director's time as well. To provide a contemporary program that is responsive to current professional research, the field director is constantly evaluating and redesigning the field experience programs being offered. This involves a lot of literature research and qualitative and quantitative data collection. Based on this research and data, the director designs and revises program offerings, procedures, policies, and goals. Through the convening of representative committees of persons and institutions affected by field experience programs, the director facilitates and guides program decision making. At these meetings, the director is responsible for sharing the research and data that have been gathered. The committees then review the material and make their recommendations. The final responsibility for program planning rests in the hands of the director.

Program Implementation

Once the program decisions and procedures are determined, the actual implementation is the responsibility of the director. Program implementation means the planning and conducting of numerous meetings with university faculty, office staff members, public school officials, university students, public school teachers, and, many times, university administrative officers. All publics involved and/or affected by the program's operations need to be apprised of the current program in place and how it functions.

Leadership for the Office of Educational Field Experience

To keep the field experience programs running smoothly, the core unit of the office staff and professional faculty must function as a cohesive team. This team of individuals must be mutually supportive in all endeavors for which the office of field experiences is responsible. It is, therefore, the major responsibility of the director to create this team atmosphere and do everything possible to maintain it. Careful consideration must be given to the selection and hiring of office staff. They must be able to function effectively as team members. They should be flexible, positive individuals who are able to deal with the various publics with whom they will come in contact. The field director must strive to create a feeling of individual worth among all the staff and faculty. Each should appreciate the other and respect the specific contributions of each individual. Just as the director uses transformational leadership with all the publics the office serves, he or she should incorporate the same style of leadership with the office staff and faculty directly responsible for the implementation of the field experience programs.

Along with the responsibility of hiring personnel comes the additional responsibility of evaluating and, if necessary, terminating employees. The latter may be avoided by proceeding carefully during the hiring stage. The director should view each employee of the field experience office as an individual whose professional skills can grow and develop. Therefore, whenever possible, the director should provide the resources and opportunities for staff and faculty to participate in staff development and/or professional conferences. If the director's repertoire includes expertise in areas of staff development that the office employees need, then he/she may provide the staff development. The typical field experience office will employ secretarial and clerical staff and often an assistant director as well. Some programs have full-time faculty members assigned to the field experience office whose academic assignment is to supervise students in the field. In addition, some offices employ their own faculty for field supervision. Student work-study personnel and an occasional graduate assistant (assigned for a particular research project) round out the total staff for which a director is responsible. Suffice it to say that the director must work with numerous people who are under his or her direct supervision.

Fiscal Management

The field director is the signature authority for program operational expenditures. The fiscal management of a field experience office generally includes both a personnel budget and an operational budget. Personnel would include secretarial, clerical, and work-study staff, as well as administrative assistant(s) and supervisory faculty who are assigned permanently to the field experience unit. Operational budgets typically include such line items as wages, commodities, expenses incurred through contract agreements (e.g., telephone), and travel. In most field experience programs, other than salaries, travel is the largest budget item. It is the field director's responsibility to very carefully budget the amount provided. There generally will be a monthly printout provided by the business office with which to check expenditures and balances. Careful watch over the budget is a must if the program and the director are to be considered viable.

Staff Development

Another aspect of training for which the director is responsible is the ongoing staff development of all faculty. To remain abreast of program changes and to proceed proactively with state-of-the-art programs, the faculty involved in implementing such programs must be trained to appropriately implement them. The director either conducts this training or arranges for it to be done. A field experience university supervisor must deal with adult learners, most of the time in a one-on-one situation. This means that these university professors must have effective skills in teaching adult learners. The university supervisors must clearly understand the dynamics of subjective and objective interaction with another professional adult. They must be effective communicators, professional role models, and personal counselors for the adults they are guiding through stages of professional development. The field director must emphasize the importance of the university supervisor in the overall preparation of preservice teachers. It is advisable that the field director provide training in supervision and adult learning strategies for both the university supervisor and the public school cooperating teachers. It is a well-known fact that cooperating teachers may be excellent classroom teachers, but that does not guarantee they will be able to effectively fulfill the role of mentor for neophyte teachers. Staff development training directed toward improving mentoring skills may be offered through workshops, college credit courses, or district-sponsored staff development options. Ultimately, the type and content of the training programs will need to be designed, initiated, and implemented by the field director.

Field Participation

A conscientious field director will want to be in touch with the field experience programs in the public schools, so he or she will frequently visit field sites to see, first hand, how the programs are functioning in the field. Sometimes the director's purpose is to observe the university faculty in action. At other times, it is advisable for the director to supervise several students in the field. This helps the director keep in touch with the students' needs during field experiences. One of the most important reasons for the field director to visit field experience sites is to meet and visit with cooperating teachers, principals, and school district central office administrators. Through informal meetings and discussions, the field director will have the opportunity to learn about the public school personnel's perceptions of the success of the field experience programs in that district.

Special Events

The celebration of success is a part of most accomplishments. So it is with field experiences as well. One of the nicest ways to say thank you to the professionals who make the field experience programs a success is to sponsor special events that honor those individuals. This may take the form of a banquet or luncheon with a featured speaker of professional renown. Receptions with specialty foods, teaching material door prizes, and individual gift packs for everyone attending make for a good time for all. Some universities provide tuition-free courses for cooperating teachers who have served field experience programs over a period of time. The organizing and execution of such special recognition events and privileges are the responsibility of the field director.

Conclusion

The field director wears many hats in order to develop, maintain, evaluate, and celebrate the field experience programs provided by his or her university. First and foremost, the director's resolve must be to promote the integrity and quality of the teacher education programs at his or her university. The director must work diligently to establish positive working relationships with all the various publics that are affected by the field experience programs. Collaboration and effective communication are the keys to that success.

References

Patterson, J. L. (1993). *Leadership for tomorrow's schools*. Alexandria, VA: Association for Supervision and Curriculum Development.

Slick, G. A., & Gupton, S. (1993). *Systemic change in education: Inclusivity of women in leadership roles*. Paper presented at the Southeast Regional Association of Teacher Educators, Nashville, TN.

❖ 2 ❖

Organizing and Managing Field Experience Programs

CHARLES E. JAQUITH

Traditionally, "field experience program" has been another name for student teaching. In recent years, field experience programs have come to include early contact hours with children or clinical experiences, some sort of practicum or mid-tier field experience often associated with methods classes, and the student teaching or internship semester. This chapter considers the organization and management of three levels of field experiences.

Mission Statement

The mission of field experience programs is to provide systematic and realistic contacts between teacher education students and the tasks involved in teaching in K-12 classrooms for the purposes of:

1. Creating awareness of differences in teaching at various levels and in regular and special education.
2. Finding ways to apply the theories and methods learned in professional education classes.
3. Experimenting with and developing teaching practices that individual student teachers can use when they have their own classrooms.
4. Screening out individuals who are not capable of performing successfully in a classroom.

Variables Affecting the Operation of Field Experience Programs

Placements

There are differences in the locus of field experiences in teacher education programs. Initial field experience programs are usually housed within a teacher education department and occur prior to admittance to teacher education programs. Frequently, the field experience director arranges school placements and, with professional education faculty, establishes performance tasks for students in early level field programs. Professional education faculty often arrange placements and supervise the performance of elementary mid-tier students, and faculty in the academic methods classes often supervise secondary students during their mid-tier experiences. The placement of student teachers is the responsibility of the field experience director, and supervision of student teachers is handled by teacher education faculty and/or instructors from the academic disciplines. In some universities, all professional education classes, including the field experience, occur after prospective teachers have earned their baccalaureate degrees.

The numbers of teacher education students needing field experiences at any given time and the numbers of quality placements available in schools close to the university control the distribution of students for placement in field experiences. In areas with high population density, this is not a problem; field experience directors in rural or low population density areas have to be creative in arranging field experience placements. Students involved in introductory or mid-tier field experiences typically are also enrolled in on-campus classes, so their field experiences must be close to the university. Because student teachers are in schools full-time, their placements tend to be farther away.

Teacher education students need placements with outstanding teachers who can serve as role models. The increased emphasis on field experiences has resulted in new partnerships between universities and local schools and the establishment of "professional development schools," organized in such a way that universities provide professional development activities for teachers, and teachers provide quality placements for teacher education students (Duffy, 1994, p. 596). This type of arrangement makes possible a continuity among the three levels of preservice educational field experiences.

Supervision

High-quality university supervisors are critical to the success of field experience programs. Supervisors need solid academic and pedagogical backgrounds as well as successful teaching experience at the level of the students they are supervising. They need to be able to demonstrate enthusiasm, love of working with young people, and genuine pride in the teaching profession.

University supervisors should also hold professorial appointments with their employing university in order to maintain credibility with cooperating teachers, school administrators, the on-campus faculty, and their own students. When university supervisors have responsibilities for conducting seminars or field-based classes, a full load of student teachers should not exceed 18 students (NCATE, 1994, Standard IIIC, p. 13) in order to allow them to observe and evaluate their students at least every other week.

Pre-Student Teaching Field Experiences

Often students enroll in higher education institutions having made no career decisions or having made decisions based on inadequate information. Many teacher preparation institutions have responded by offering an Introduction to Teaching class that incorporates a field or clinical experience component that requires systematic structured observations of teacher roles in a variety of school settings and levels (NCATE, 1994, Standard IH, p. 7). Most send students into schools for observations, and others use either videotapes of actual classroom performances or interactive computer simulation situations.

The Introduction to Teaching classes provide students with a realistic basis for deciding whether to pursue a career as a teacher, and if the answer is yes, in what disciplines and at what levels the student desires to teach. To accomplish these objectives, a director of field experience needs to work closely with personnel from nearby K-12 schools to organize procedures for identifying placement locations, arranging methods for the selection of host teachers and the assignment of teacher education students, describing the tasks that the students will be expected to complete, and clarifying the responsibilities of host teachers and the Introduction to Teaching instructors. Sometimes these tasks are performed by the Introduction to Teaching instructors.

Developing Early Field Experience Programs

A first step is a meeting with district administrators of school systems close to the university to describe the mission of the program and to solicit their suggestions and support. The idea of early screening of potential teachers appeals to administrators and they like having an extra pair of "no cost" helping hands in the classrooms. This meeting provides an opportunity to create an advisory council composed of teachers, building administrators, and university representatives. The council would be charged with the task of writing guidelines and a timetable for implementing the program. Teachers and administrators need to have ownership of the program and see benefits to the profession or they will begin to raise the question of compensation for allowing students to come into their buildings.

Most Introduction to Teaching programs include lecture/discussion sections aimed at introducing students to the structures and functions of education at various levels. Many successful programs pay for substitute teachers in order to release teachers and/or principals to appear as guest speakers.

Implementing Early Experience Programs

Typically, students are required to spend at least 15 hours observing classrooms at the elementary, middle school, and senior high levels in regular education, and at least one type of special education program. They are asked to record the social behaviors of students, classroom management strategies of teachers, typical interruptions of the school day, the types of learning activities, the use of time, the availability of auxiliary resources, teacher involvement with parents, extracurricular activities, and the advantages and disadvantages of teaching at each level. These written observations are evaluated by the Introduction to Teaching instructors and then placed in the professional portfolios of the students.

Host teachers are asked to respond to questions of the students and to assign tasks appropriate for the untrained students. They also keep track of the dates and times a university student was in their room and have the option of writing a letter of commendation for students who seem have the potential for becoming good teachers. The responsibility for assigning a grade rests with the university instructors. Critical to the success of early experience programs is a provision for removing students who are disruptive to classroom activities. Students who discover early in the semester that they do not want to become teachers should be able to withdraw from the field component and earn course credit based on completing the academic portions of the class. Another critical factor is that university instructors need to visit at least once with each of the teachers who are hosting university students.

The Mid-Tier Field Experience Program

Mid-tier field experience programs provide students with opportunities to experience activities relevant to their preparation. At the time a student is ready to register in the mid-tier experience, the student should have completed most general education requirements and a large proportion of the major/minor requirements, passed mandated tests of basic skills, been admitted to teacher education, and completed some of the professional education classes. These students should be ready for more teacher-oriented tasks than they were at the time of their initial field experience. In many institutions the mid-tier field experience is part of a methods class taught by instructors in specific academic disciplines for secondary-level education students or of methods courses taught by education faculty for elementary-level education students.

Most universities that provide mid-tier field experiences require their students to spend at least 45 clock hours in a classroom at their certification level (Jaquith, 1991). Secondary-level students frequently spend this time in middle school or senior high classrooms that match their academic majors and/or minors. Elementary-level students spend this time in elementary or middle school grades, working in a variety of subject areas (Jaquith, 1994). There seems to be no consistent pattern for how the mid-tier experiences are used between or even within universities. The variations range from 3 hours a week for 15 weeks to all day during university holidays.

Implementing the Mid-Tier Field Experience Program

As with the initial field experience, implementing a mid-tier field experience means sharing ownership with K-12 teachers and administrators. Initiating a program requires a series of meetings involving the director of field experience, the mid-tier instructors from specific certification areas, elementary teachers, and teachers of subject area classes (e.g., math, English, art, science, etc.). The university representatives need to work with classroom teachers to identify the kinds of tasks (small-group instruction, whole-group instruction, tutoring, planning, assessment, etc.) mid-tier students could complete in a given time frame, desired times (of the semester and of the day) for mid-tier students to be in their rooms, and information about the content of the classes the mid-tier students will be involved in teaching.

Placement of Mid-Tier Students

The information collected from the planning sessions can be recorded on data cards and made available to students wishing to register for the mid-tier experience. Students should register for assignment to mid-tier placement early in the semester prior to the semester of the experience. This allows them to coordinate the times for the mid-tier experience with their class schedules. Students complete application forms with information about their preparation and background, and these are mailed to the school prior to the interview day. At the interview with the principal and host teacher, details are worked out concerning the mid-tier experience. Generally, schools reserve the right to not accept a student whom they feel might not fit in with their program. If this occurs, the director of field experience assists the student in finding a different school placement.

Assessing Mid-Tier Students

Students are expected to complete tasks such as developing bulletin boards, working with individual students and small groups, correcting homework and tests, teaching and assessing lessons, assisting the teacher in preparing teaching materials, and the like. The host teachers keep a record of tasks completed and share this information with mid-tier instructors when they visit in the schools. Assessment of student performance is primarily the responsibility of mid-tier instructors, but the mid-tier instructors receive input from host teachers concerning the quality of student performance. These assessments become part of a student's professional portfolio.

Mid-tier instructors occasionally come into classes and teach demonstration lessons, or they may substitute for the host teacher.

This frees the host teacher to speak to on-campus education classes. Mid-tier instructors can also be available to assist local schools with curriculum improvement projects and often organize regional activities, such as contests, festivals, or special days. Mid-tier instructors should meet frequently with host teachers in their subject matter field for assessment of the mid-tier program and to develop cooperative activities.

The Student Teaching or Internship Experience

The major purposes of the student teaching semester are providing time in a realistic setting for students to gain experiences in implementing skills and knowledge they will need to become successful teachers, and serving as an assessment of student's readiness for entering the teaching profession. Most students view student teaching as the most significant learning experience in their professional preparation, and most administrators consider the student teaching assessment as the most important document in the portfolios of teacher candidates.

Preparation for Student Teaching

Because it is such an important experience, it is necessary to carefully prepare students for student teaching and to systematically screen the applicants. Most field experience directors schedule a mass meeting for education students early in the semester prior to student teaching to distribute application forms, review the requirements for admission to student teaching, and explain the procedures for assigning students to field sites. The application forms provide a basis for screening the students and also provide potential cooperating teachers with information to help them decide whether to accept a particular student teacher.

Most universities specify the following as criteria for admission to student teaching: a minimum grade point average; completion of specified courses in the academic major and minor, and in the professional education sequence; and evidence of having a mastery of basic knowledge and skills. A number of institutions review the professional portfolios of education students as a basis for determining readiness for student teaching.

Placing Student Teachers

Some institutions allow students to have a voice in the location of their student teaching placements, but others flatly state that assignments will be within driving distance of the campus. The entry of increasing numbers of nontraditional students with wide-ranging family situations has resulted in more demands for flexibility in school assignments. Sometimes these problems can be alleviated by cooperative agreements in which a university agrees to supervise student teachers from a university in another area. It is important that "guest student teaching" arrangements be made by field experience directors and not by students, in order to ensure that the reasons for special consideration are valid and that all entry requirements have been satisfied. Students sometimes fail to realize that a 10-week experience at a university on the quarter system does not necessarily generate the credits needed in an institution with a 16-week semester. Most schools that accept "guest" student teachers charge a fee to the student that ranges from $100 up to full tuition (Jaquith, 1994).

Most universities require a full semester of all-day student teaching, but there are variances in how the semester is used. Traditionally, a student teacher was assigned to work under one cooperating teacher for a full semester, because it was felt that a semester was barely enough time to master the skills needed for entry to student teaching. Since the implementation of multilevel field experience programs, there is a strong tendency to diversify the assignments so that placements more closely represent the employment opportunities available to students upon graduation. Elementary and secondary education students might student teach a half-semester in a middle school; secondary level students might experience a half-semester in their major and another in their minor. Possible combinations for student teaching placements are shown in Table 2.1.

The rationale for variable placement arrangements is that because of earlier field experiences, students more quickly adapt

TABLE 2.1 Student Teaching Placement Options

Certification	1st Half Term	2nd Half Term
Elementary	— Early elementary or prekindergarten	— Upper elementary
	— Urban or suburban	— Suburban or urban
	— Middle elementary	— Middle school
Secondary Students may work part-time in elementary, middle school, and senior highs when working on K-12 certification. (Art, P.E., Music, etc.)	— Senior high major	— Middle school minor
	— Senior high major & minor	— Middle school major and/or minor
	— Urban or suburban	— Suburban or urban

NOTE: States that have separate certificates for middle school may require options different from those shown in the table.

to working in new settings, and although a half-term is a shorter time, students will grow professionally, and diversity in student teaching experience enhances employability of prospective teachers. The key to successful student teaching experiences is placements with *exemplary* cooperating teachers. Placement of student teachers with inadequate cooperating teachers because "the experience might help the cooperating teacher to improve" is *never a good reason for a placement.* Students need experience working in culturally diverse situations and in schools *different* from those they attended. Whenever possible, more than one student teacher should be placed in a school, not only so they can provide each other with mutual support but also to reduce the time a university supervisor spends in driving between schools.

It is important for the student teacher to meet with the principal(s) and cooperating teacher(s) of the school(s) to which the student has been assigned early in the semester, *before* the field experience is scheduled, to clarify the materials that will be taught during student teaching. This meeting should also serve as a two-way screening process to determine whether the student teacher and cooperating teacher are compatible and if the student teacher will fit in with the school program. No teacher should feel compelled to accept a student teacher. Selection of cooperating teachers is improved when university representatives establish an advisory committee involving teachers' and administrators' help in establishing guidelines for field experience programs. Involvement in developing guidelines leads to a feeling of ownership that is critical to a successful student teaching program. Universities have a professional responsibility to provide training for cooperating teachers and administrators.

Supervising Student Teachers

Because student teaching is critically important, one might expect teacher training institutions to assign their best faculty to supervise student teachers. A survey of staffing practices (Jaquith, 1994) reveals that supervision is frequently done by graduate students, retired teachers, or principals, or as a part-time responsibility of teaching professors. University supervisors need both a solid academic preparation in educational theory and experience as a teacher or a school administrator. Because university supervisors often provide academic counseling to teachers or teach graduate-level classes, they should meet the requirements for graduate faculty in their institutions. In some states, university supervisors have a mentoring role in new teacher induction.

The *NCATE Evaluative Criteria* require supervisors of student teachers to be certified at the level of the students they are supervising (NCATE, 1994, Standard IIIA, pp. 11-12). Universities that utilize supervisors from the academic disciplines are generally able to provide a match between the majors of the student teachers and the preparation of the supervisors, but sometimes the supervisors do not hold teaching certificates. To resolve this situation, a number of institutions use certified professors of teacher education to do most of the supervision and "purchase time" from the academic departments so that they can visit students from their disciplines at least twice a semester to be sure the subject matter being taught is accurate and appropriate. Few students fail student teaching because they are weak in subject matter, but having the subject matter specialists get out into the schools enables them to be better informed concerning current issues and practices in the schools.

University supervisors need to regularly go to the schools of their student teachers to observe the student teachers' activities, assess the quality of the performance, and confer with the student teachers and the cooperating teachers. Written copies of observation notes should be provided to the students and to the cooperating teachers. An open and cooperative relationship is essential to promoting growth in student teachers. Student teachers should be encouraged to do reflective self-evaluation, but the university supervisor must offer clear suggestions, to the student teacher and the cooperating teacher, concerning what the student is doing well and what should be done to improve. The university supervisor and the cooperating teacher need to confer regularly concerning the progress of the student so that the written final evaluation does not contain surprises.

Student Teacher Issues

A major issue concerning student teachers is whether they can be used as substitute teachers. There are times when the student teacher needs to work with students without having the cooperating teacher in the room, but a cooperating teacher needs to be available to provide help in the event of a crisis. A student teacher should not be allowed to substitute for another teacher. If a cooperating teacher has to be absent for a short time, *and* if the student teacher and the cooperating teacher feel the student teacher is ready to work alone, *and* if the principal is willing to designate someone to act as a cooperating teacher, a student teacher may be allowed to take full charge of the classroom during the absence of the regular cooperating teacher. Because they are receiving university credit for the experience, it is unethical and a conflict of interest for student teachers to be paid for doing this.

Sometimes student teachers may have received more training in some aspects of pedagogy than their cooperating teachers. This is particularly true regarding technologies such as E-mail, computerized bulletin boards, and networking. If the school has the equipment, this is an excellent opportunity for the student teacher and university supervisor to assist a school faculty with professional development activities. This can be a positive experience for all who are involved and should be provided at no charge to the school.

Assessment of Student Teachers

Using professional portfolios as part of the process for evaluating student teachers has become an increasingly widespread practice. Traditionally, checklist rating sheets and/or structured anecdotal comments have been used to report student teacher performance, but employing officials are increasingly requesting documentation of readiness to teach. The evaluation form has become one of many documents in a comprehensive portfolio that is replacing the old "teaching credentials."

Not everyone who is admitted to student teaching will be successful, so it is necessary to have policies and procedures for dealing with marginal students. Because student teachers have met the requirements for admission to the program, professional educators must do all in their power to enable student teachers to have a successful experience. When it appears that a student teacher is having problems, the university supervisor and the cooperating teacher need to work with the student teacher in developing a plan of action to improve the student's classroom performance. These plans need to include deadlines for completing specified activities and clearly defined criteria for determining successful completion of each activity. These plans should be recorded in writing along with information the problem(s) that resulted in formulating an action plan. This information should be shared with the director of field experience.

If the plan does not appear to be succeeding, the director may come to the school for an observation and conferences with the student teacher, the cooperating teacher, and the university supervisor. At this point, the student's placement might be changed or the student teacher might be removed and assigned specific tasks that must be completed successfully before the student teaching experience can be restarted. If the situation is so serious that all involved feel the student lacks the potential to become a teacher, the student should be withdrawn from the program and provided with counseling concerning alternative careers.

It is *essential* for complete records to be kept that document the efforts made to assist the student and evidence that the student was not successful in responding to the assistance. Written notes of observations, videotapes of the student teacher in action, and copies of the action plan are the kinds of evidence needed if the student decides to question the decision in court.

Managerial Considerations for Field Experience Programs

Finances

The nature of field experience programs tends to result in higher costs than on-campus classes. Student teachers are usually expected to provide their own housing, meals, and transportation, but university supervisors are usually reimbursed for mileage and meals. The amount of money paid as honoraria to cooperating teachers varies greatly but usually ranges between $25 and $300 per semester. Some universities pay a lower honorarium but provide tuition-free classes to cooperating teachers and administrators. This is often an incentive for increasing enrollment in classes dealing with supervision of student teachers.

Communications

Communications are vitally important but often result in considerable expense to the field program; however, inadequate communications result in a flood of problems. Long-distance phone calls are being replaced by faxing and E-mail, but the costs are still high. Well-written handbooks and the use of mass meetings help to clarify the roles and responsibilities of all who are involved in the field program. Clearly printed directions on observation and evaluation forms help to reduce the need for additional communications. Some universities circulate periodic newsletters, describing new practices in the schools to cooperating teachers and administrators. These can be circulated to on-campus faculty, who can be given the opportunity to write descriptive articles concerning new programs. These newsletters develop feelings of pride and tend to draw campus and field personnel closer together. It is also helpful for the director of field experience to regularly get out into the schools to visit with cooperating teachers and administrators and with field supervisors.

Field experience programs need to utilize carefully written contracts that specify conditions for placement of students in field experiences, selection of cooperating teachers, honorarium arrangements, and provisions concerning liability and coverage for injuries suffered on the job. University and local school attorneys need to be involved to be sure that agreements are in compliance with school policies and state laws. Sometimes the development of contract language will involve participation of local education associations.

Some universities require students to show evidence that they are covered with health and accident insurance as a condition for admission to field experience programs. It is important that students be thoroughly briefed concerning methods for dealing with the disposal of body fluids. Some school districts require students to have physical examinations prior to admitting them to work in their schools.

Concluding Remarks

Many of the issues mentioned in this chapter are discussed at greater length elsewhere in this book or in other books in this series. If readers have questions or desire further information, I invite them to communicate with me.

References

Duffy, G. G. (1994, April). Professional development schools and the disempowerment of teachers and professors. *Phi Delta Kappan*, pp. 596-600.

Jaquith, C. E. (1991, February). *A survey of field experience programs.* Paper presented at the meeting of National Field Directors' Forum, Los Angeles.

Jaquith, C. E. (1994). *National field directors' summer survey.* Paper presented at the Association of Teacher Educators Summer Workshop, Pittsburgh.

National Council for the Accreditation of Teacher Education (NCATE). (1994, May). *NCATE evaulative criteria.* Chicago: Author.

❖ 3 ❖

Placing Students
in Field Experiences

EDWARD M. VERTUNO

Each year, fall and spring, the miracle occurs.

The Challenge

In spite of bad press, often difficult working conditions, and seeming lack of public support, hundreds and hundreds of fledgling teachers appear at our office doors, seeking placement for their student teaching experience. Idealistic, filled with all manner of textbook theory, and inspired by their professors, they're more than a little eager to test themselves in our version of the real world, America's classrooms. How do we do it?

In each instance, the challenge is the same. We need to find appropriate placements for these soon-to-be fellow professionals: placements that will be professionally challenging, but manage-

29

able; nurturing, but not smothering; and enriched by supervising teachers eager to help renew our profession by sharing their expertise with others.

In most instances, the challenge to the institution is somewhat limited by geography and numbers. At Florida State University (FSU) the task is magnified by several factors: (a) a local school system, moderately sized, asked to serve two in-town university teacher preparation programs; (b) the number involved, approximately 550 placements per year for the past 10 years; and (c) the acceptance by FSU of a statewide mission to place interns throughout the state of Florida. What to do?

The First Step

One starts with outstanding candidates, crisply and efficiently offering themselves via applications that highlight their academic records, personal essays, and any special circumstances to be considered. The application is the primary instrument for all actions taken at every level of the placement process. It must be clean, accurate, and complete.

At FSU: The applications are printed locally, purchased by the students as part of an intern packet. Each is reviewed at the departmental level before being submitted to the Office of Student Teaching. A final check is done by our field coordinators before they submit them to the districts.

The Second Step

All prospective interns should be fully briefed as to the steps inherent in the placement process and the experience itself. Emphasis should be placed upon the need to respect the organizational structures of the districts. Students should be counseled to resist the temptation to try to arrange their own placements. They must be patient with the placement process, especially in the larger districts, but with the knowledge that our student teaching coordinators, in cooperation with district-level supervisors and school principals, are carefully seeking the finest possible placement for each of them.

At FSU: Initial placement recommendations begin with university department program personnel. These are followed by a general briefing and further recommendations by the Office of Student Teaching. Attendance is required. The entire placement process is once again reviewed, initial assignments by county are announced, and the steps to appeal that choice of county (district) assignment are outlined.

FSU has a University Student Teaching Appeals Committee, which reviews requests for placement outside our designated placement areas. Such appeals are usually based upon financial need, special circumstances of family relationship, and the like.

The Third Step

As indicated earlier, the process of placement begins as university departmental contacts meet with Office of Student Teaching personnel to recommend placements. Sometimes the placement is school- and teacher-specific; other times only the district is identified. But once requested placements are identified, the process is quickly put into full swing.

Applications are forwarded to the district officers in charge of placement. In Florida, these carry a variety of titles: Director of Staff Development, Director of Professional Orientation Program, Coordinator of Student Services, and so on. No matter the title, someone at the district level is responsible for handling the many requests for placement.

At FSU, these district-level colleagues work very closely with our university field coordinators, but with our awareness that they have a host of other district duties in addition to that which concerns us, intern placement. Indeed, even that task is often complicated by simultaneous requests from many other colleges and universities, all seeking placements in a particular district. Attention to details, such as the deadline for receiving applications, and unique district requirements are all important considerations. More and more districts are adding to the list of required information. Some now require prospective interns to complete their applications with fingerprint records, felony disclosure statements, extra transcripts, statements of commitment to the state's Code of Ethics, and so on. If these requirements are not addressed, any or all omissions lead only to delay and, sometimes, rejection of the placement requested.

The placement process must be a truly cooperative effort with the university. The placement process can be enhanced and made more efficient if we are able to offer specific suggestions as to the school and supervising teachers desired. All parties benefit if such information is shared as part of the process. This effort requires that departmental program contacts, indeed all faculty involved in the process, maintain a strong liaison effort with their colleagues in the field. They need to know them, their strengths and weaknesses, and they need to be seen as a partner in the process with the teacher in the school. Finally, they will need to make some evaluation as to the advisability of continued use of specific school-level supervising teachers and university supervisors.

All parties to the placement process must keep in mind the salient fact that participation of the schools and individual cooperating teachers is voluntary. University placement officers are aware of this, or should be. All too often, prospective interns are not. Consequently, they frequently become upset or angry if their hoped for placement is not forthcoming. But they must realize that the school is under no obligation to accept placement and may reject any or all requests for reasons related to the best interests of the school or district, for example, lack of qualified cooperating teachers, recent excessive intern load, parental concerns, school or departmental concerns that have priority, competing placement requests from other institutions, and so on. Effective communication among all participants will help ameliorate the impact of these problems and will assist in solving most of them.

At FSU: Our statewide mission creates a special set of challenges to our whole placement process. It demands that we seek placements in 24 counties (districts) in five targeted areas in the state: Area I, Tallahassee and surrounding counties; Area II, the Panhandle; Area III, Central Florida; Area IV, Tampa and vicinity; and Area V, the Lower East Coast. Such a broad directive cannot be handled from a single office hidden away on the home campus. It calls for a specific university presence in each area. Our presence, the presence of the Office of Student Teaching, is embodied in the person of the area coordinator.

The area coordinator is a full-time resident supervisor/placement officer representing the university in the areas mentioned above. Selected after a public search procedure, each is an experienced educator appointed at the rank of assistant professor. They partake of all the usual benefits associated with university employment, save tenure.

The keys to their success include their knowledge of the local area, their communication networks up and down the chain of command, and their willingness to become personally involved in the placement effort. Often their willingness to "walk it through" has saved many an application, even one submitted at the 11th hour.

The Fourth Step

The selection of the cooperating teacher is one of those signal activities upon which the success of the whole enterprise rests. It is a critical part of the whole intern experience. Carefully done, it creates the conditions for eventual success; hastily conceived, it may lead to failure.

Each should be recommended by the principal or other appropriate administrator. Each should be a willing participant in the intern program. Each should be willing to accept the responsibility for providing the necessary supervision, guidance, and evaluation of the student teacher. Each should be willing to file the usual reports and other necessary paperwork associated with the internship. Each should have the professional preparation necessary to help the budding professional grow.

At FSU: Here in Florida, most districts require supervising teachers to adhere to the following general criteria:

1. Three or more years of professional experience
2. Regularly certified in the target instructional area
3. Recommended by the appropriate administrator
4. Demonstrate consistently high quality performance
5. Complete training in the supervision of student teachers (coaching, conferring, observing, evaluating)

We seek cooperating teachers who will:

a. be willing models of exemplary instruction;
b. provide assistance in learning to plan for instructors;
c. provide specific suggestions for improvement;
d. provide a gradual assumption of teaching responsibilities;
e. evaluate interns as interns, not as experienced teachers;
f. demonstrate a positive attitude in working for the benefit of the student teacher;
g. provide regular reports of intern progress;
h. provide an early alert to developing problems;
i. openly and freely communicate with those concerned with intern progress;
j. support the intern in the timely completion of all responsibilities.

Of course, special circumstances may require that exceptions be made to these general requirements, but in the main, when these requirements are ignored, it often leads to difficult placements that can be traumatic for all concerned. Great care must be taken to avoid the usual pitfalls known to every placement director. These would include those placements made to resuscitate a teacher suffering burn-out, to acquire teacher aides, to free the classroom teacher for other duties, to satisfy a "debt" of sorts to a teacher or other colleague, and all placements made without the enthusiastic agreement of the potential supervising teacher.

The Fifth Step

Difficult placements are, in my judgment, relatively rare, but they do occur. Some are quite abrasive, as when the intern and the supervisor are mismatched. Perhaps it's personality, grade level, content level, and so on. Others are more subtle: overuse of a small cadre of cooperating teachers, philosophical differences, and so on. Each has its own special hazard when corrective action is contemplated. To act precipitously is to put at risk long-term relationships with the school and district involved. To delay is to risk allowing the problem to fester and grow, almost always to the detriment of the student teacher. Timing is important, but timing for what?

Placement activities are public relations of a high order. The motives are the purest: to find and provide the best possible professional experience for the student teacher. To that end, we contact and utilize many publics that serve the schools we want to use for our students. Yet each of those publics, from the district offices downtown to the department heads in the local school to the classroom teacher, will also have its own special agenda. When these agendas coincide with ours, the prognosis for the student teacher is positive; when they diverge, it is much less so. This divergence embodies all of the potential placement problems to which we have already alluded. Efforts to seek remedies must be carefully considered, because all sorts of professional and personal sensitivities may be involved. However, the potential pitfalls should not deter us from action on behalf of our students. Act we must if we are to maintain the integrity of the placement procedures and the viability of the experience for the student teacher.

These situations are never pleasant. Indeed, we often find them distasteful and often don't fully understand them. After all, common sense tells that no one should have made such a placement, said such a thing, and so on. But it has happened. How do we change it? Consider the three Cs: Contact, Communication, and Candor. Each is a vital component of any possible corrective action.

Contact: All partners in the placement process must maintain contact. Those involved in placement should make every effort to get to know the district contacts, the principals, even the teachers, as thoroughly as possible. We can't often solve problems if we remain strangers. Professional colleagues can often discover avenues for corrective action. The student teacher can only benefit when the partnership flourishes. Get out of the office, visit the schools, get to know the territory.

Communication: Be willing to share your message with all concerned. Be especially forthright in detailing your expectations of the placement, the cooperating teachers, and all other conditions that involve the student teacher. All parties need to be fully informed so they can understand and accept all that will be required of them.

Candor: Be candid in your communication. If there is a problem, state it. Try to avoid dropping hints; they are almost never taken. Subtle suggestions are most often defined by the receiver than by the sender. Be direct. Speak to the problems at hand. Do not hesitate to speak about professional problems with other professionals. If you have a prior record of contact and communication, your message should be well received even if the answer may not always be to your liking. But you must be direct.

There is a fourth C: Compromise. One can never compromise over placement conditions that might harm the student teacher or might create incompatibilities with the potential for success that must inhere to any placement. Absent that extreme, some compromise might be possible that will allow the general relationship to continue although it may vary in its particulars. One accepts a different school than the one requested, a teacher other than the one identified, or even an alternative grade level. Judged against the standard of the well-being of the student teacher, each of these could be acceptable on an ad hoc basis, acceptable for now; and by its being accepted, the long-term relationship with the teacher, the school, and the district will prosper.

At FSU: All of the foregoing are inherent in the operational expectations of our area coordinators. They must, indeed do, make strong, consistent, repetitive efforts to maintain contact with the district personnel involved in the placement process. Our travel budgets, in-house procedures, and outreach efforts all speak to persistent efforts to communicate directly with our colleagues. In moments of difficulty we want them to speak directly to the problems. No matter what the perceived risk about loss of rapport, loss of placement, and so on, we are more often than not pleasantly surprised at the response we receive when we've built upon a base of contact-communication-candor.

The area coordinator concept yields another benefit that we find most valuable. The area coordinators, in addition to serving as initiators of the placement process, also serve as field supervisors. At the elementary level they provide full supervision for those interns around the state. At the secondary level they provide at least half the scheduled supervision. In both cases, their level of contact is quite high, their opportunities to communicate many and varied, and their ability to respond to problems heightened by their proximity in time and space to problems as they arise. It makes the statewide mission viable and valuable for all concerned.

The placement challenge depends upon many factors: the numbers involved, the proximity to potential sites, the professionalism of the districts utilized, the quality of the candidates, and the overall relationship of the university to the schools it purports to serve. Given qualified candidates, the recipe for success is fairly succinct: Make frequent contact, communicate freely, be candid in adversity, and compromise within standards. Always keep the welfare of the student teacher fixed in focus. We want the miracle to occur again and again.

❖ 4 ❖

Displacing Student Teachers

The Need for Policies

JAN CROSS

The discontinuation of a student teacher's public school placement is probably the most traumatic experience for all involved in the teacher education process. Sometimes the discontinuation results from the student teacher's inability to handle the complexities of any public school classroom and comes early in the assignment. More frequently, the discontinuation results from circumstances that need to be changed for the student teacher to be successful. In this transition time, the student teacher is faced with what appears to be a failure and serious implications for future career plans. The cooperating teacher may feel personal guilt and responsibility for the placement's not working out. The university supervisor is aware of both the professional and the political impact of the need to end the placement. Historically, unsuccessful placements have included some or all of the following negative outcomes: (a) polarization of the student teacher's perceptions, (b) attempts to fix blame, (c) loss of collegial acceptance of shared professional responsibility for teacher preparation, (d) loss of the student teacher to the profession, and (e) loss of the school site for future placements.

In the most distressing placement terminations the cooperating teacher has patiently and silently tried to improve the student teacher's experiences. When the burden becomes unbearable for the cooperating teacher, a plea goes to the principal and/or the university supervisor for the immediate relief provided by removing the student teacher. Suddenly the student teacher becomes the university's problem. The crisis can then bring about finger pointing, and the student, who may have been protected from negative feedback by the cooperating teacher and university supervisor, is too distraught to make good decisions. Often the student's easy out is to decide that teaching is not a desirable occupational goal.

To prevent such negative results, the trauma of placement termination should be managed systematically *before* it becomes a crisis. This prevention is more likely if there has been a carefully developed discontinuation policy that is known to all through inclusion in a fieldwork handbook (or some other printed medium). Just as in the detailed checklist used by commercial airlines, a system of sequential steps for all to follow can bring rationality to the highly emotional situation of discontinuing a student teacher from a school placement.

Development of a
Program's Discontinuation Policy

The following major assumption should be the basis for establishing a discontinuation policy:

Preparation of teachers is a responsibility shared by the faculties and administrators of both the public school and the university. Central to this responsibility is collaboration in the arrangement for classroom placement of student teachers and in any subsequent discontinuation that might become necessary during or at the end of a semester. Always every effort is made to ensure the best fit within each student teacher's placement.

But how is it collaboratively possible to individualize student teaching assignments, especially in a large program? Realistically, this goal of matching a student teacher to the best classroom setting may not be met in each placement. However, the university field placement director or the faculty responsible for placement will want to develop, with school district personnel, workable guidelines that ensure collaboration whenever possible.

Informal evaluation of school sites and classrooms for placements by university supervisors and public school administrators is a long-standing tradition and practice. However, the very informality of this process, and even its secrecy, has done little to help when a placement needs to be terminated. When the initial placement was not made through consultation, the student's failing often results in the cooperating teacher's feeling that the student was not well prepared, or that the site administrator was not supportive, or that the university supervisor did not visit often enough. The university supervisor is likely to look at the failed placement as resulting from lack of skill on the cooperating teacher's part. The informal evaluation is then concluded, with the supervisor or the site administrator vowing never to place another student in *that* classroom.

In contrast, a team evaluation of a classroom's potential for a specific student in serious difficulty moves the evaluation from an informal assessment of the cooperating teacher to a close look at the fit between student and placement. The evaluation by the team for best fit results in a candid but not threatening assessment of the appropriateness of the classroom. The decision not to put a student in a particular classroom simply means that the setting does not meet the student's unique needs. Since the teacher is participating as a member of the team, the emphasis is on what the classroom has to offer and not the skill of the teacher. The placement decision is a group decision and, if it does not work out, the termination is also a group decision.

Actual Policy

A policy, once developed jointly by university and public school teacher educators, should be written concisely as a one-page checklist that establishes step-by-step procedures before discontinuation becomes the final decision. The procedures provide a time sequence for, and key persons to be involved in, the discussions of the student's performance and the suitability of the placement. Actions each party is to take before discontinuation are specified. This procedure should soothe the participants, bring some objectivity to the problem, and protect the rights of all participants. Most of the following checklist items would be appropriate pieces of a discontinuation policy that assures a sequential attempt to solve student teaching problems:

- The university supervisor, the cooperating teacher(s), and the site administrator meet to assess concerns raised about a weak student teaching experience. (Criterion: Is the placement a good fit for the student teacher?)

- The team reviews the written feedback already provided to the student teacher by the supervisor, the cooperating teacher, and the administrator, plus their suggestions for improving the teaching performance. They decide on an action plan with required changes and a time line for making them. (Criteria: Did the team give adequate written feedback on classroom performance to the student teacher? Was the student teacher made aware of resources at the public school site and university campus that could help make the placement successful?)

- The team confers immediately with the student teacher to be sure that he or she is aware of the seriousness of the situation; to listen to the student's viewpoint about the assignment; and to share the above action plan and its time line, with incorporation of new ideas and perceptions from the student teacher. (Criterion: Did the team work out with the student a plan and time line for improving classroom performance?)

- At the designated point on the time line for assessment of improvement, the team meets again to share more observation and progress data. One of the following three decisions is made at this point: (a) the student teacher's progress has been satisfactory and continuous; therefore, the placement continues; *or* (b) the student teacher's efforts demonstrate some progress, but the placement does not allow for enough progress for continuation in this classroom; therefore, a new placement is recommended; *or* (c) the student teacher's skills are not improving enough that competencies can be met by semester's end or ever; *therefore*, another placement is not recommended. Note: If the safety of the students is a concern, the termination of the placement may have to be immediate. (Criterion: Has the student been given ample opportunity to implement the plan with adequate support?)

- The student teacher is informed of the team's decision, both in writing and in a conference. (Criterion: Should the current placement be terminated, and if so, should another student teaching experience be recommended?)

- If the team recommends another classroom assignment, it develops, with the student teacher, a description of an assignment that will be a better fit and decides when that new placement could start.

- If the team recommends that the student teacher not be provided a second placement, it will discuss with the student other career alternatives and available supporting campus resources. The student is also informed of the possibility of appeal.

- The team should review the reasons for the unsatisfactory placement. If the classroom circumstances are such that any student teacher would have had difficulty in succeeding, future placements will probably not be made there. In the discussion of this classroom as a future placement, care should be taken to assess the attributes of the classroom rather than the cooperating teacher's skills.

Rationale for Either New Placement or
Withdrawal of the Student Teacher From the Program

"Should the student be given another assignment?" is often the most difficult question for the team to answer. If the answer is affirmative, the placement process begins again after the team conference with the student about the reasons for the discontinuation. If more than 6 weeks of the semester have passed, a second placement usually would not be made until the subsequent semester. If the answer is negative and another placement is not recommended, the team will want to discuss the reasons with the student, using a humane strategy that may include referrals for career and personal counseling. At least one team member may wish to continue as a mentor to the student.

If all has gone well to this point, the student teacher will move toward reflective acceptance of the team's decision that continuing toward a career in teaching is not advisable. However, the unaccepting student teacher may eventually insist on appealing this decision. An appropriate body for such an appeal is a committee that hears student appeals about admissions and continuing program decisions. An appeals committee might be composed of dean-appointed faculty, both from credential programs and from departments that prepare students in their undergraduate teaching majors (liberal studies, math, and so on). In a meeting of the appeals committee with the student teacher, the procedure of appeal might progress in this way: (a) the student teacher expands the written reasons on an appeal form for requesting another student teaching opportunity, and then answers questions from the appeals committee members; (b) one member of the team presents in person the reasons for discontinuation and answers questions of the appeals committee; (c) written records (observations, evaluations) are examined by the committee, if so requested; and (d) members decide to grant or not grant the student's appeal. The chair of the appeals committee then advises the student of the decision and shares the committee's thinking, when appropriate. Such an appeals committee experience should provide some additional faculty insights for the student teacher to process.

Written Documentation

Written documentation of teaching performance is extremely important, regardless of whether a student's performance is successful or borderline. Particularly when observers become concerned about the overall lack of student teaching competence, they must begin to share, concretely and systematically, with the student teacher those problems that need to be corrected before the semester's student teaching credit is earned. Oral communication is not enough; the student teacher must have written suggestions to refer to frequently. He or she would benefit from seeing the written patterns develop from observation to observation. Below is a sample of a pre-midterm summary documentation by a university supervisor, the member of the team responsible for the grade, who ultimately recommends this student teacher's discontinuation from the teacher preparation program. Harsh and detailed as this documentation may seem, its purpose is to help the student teacher see his teaching from points of view other than his own.

> This memorandum serves as a pre-midterm evaluation of your student teaching assignment in _____ (cooperating teacher's name) third-grade class at _____ School. Field observations and conferences result in my informing you that certain important competencies must be improved significantly to ensure your continuance in the program. This memo itemizes both the areas in which you demonstrate appropriate progress at this point and areas in which improvement is required.

Then continues the supervisor's listing of areas in which progress has been satisfactory. Next are listed problem areas clustered in competency groups, based on the referenced state guidelines, for planning, procedures, and professional/personal characteristics. Included below is an excerpt from the procedures section, written by the supervisor.

In implementing these lessons, you used one teaching strategy: lecture/recitation, with information written on the overhead projector. You did approximately 95% of the talking during any lesson. Questions directed to students were often answered by you before the students would respond. Additionally, directions given to students for work they were to do were usually unclear and incomplete. In the last lesson I observed you teach, the majority of students did not know what they were expected to do, and though several did eventually discover what was assigned, one third of the class never did accurately complete the assignment. Lessons generally were not adapted to the needs or interests of the students nor did the lessons elicit inquiry from the students. (Various CTC competencies not yet met were cited.)

When concluding statements of such a memorandum occur at the time of a final decision, the instructor of record makes clear whether he or she does or does not recommend a repeat of student teaching, and if not, the reasons. In the above student's case, the university supervisor eventually wrote:

I do not recommend that _____ repeat Phase II for the following reasons:

1. Lack of overall progress made during the semester in the areas indicated above.
2. Expectation that progress in these areas would continue to be limited because of _____ lack of demonstration of change this semester when specific problem areas were indicated and discussed.

Summary

Even though a sound, workable discontinuation policy has been established in a teacher preparation program and is operating successfully, at some time it will be tested by a new and difficult case. As a result of such challenges and changing personnel, a discontinuation policy may need to be reconsidered fairly frequently. This reconsideration process itself may well be valuable and renewing for the collaborative team.

All faculty and administrators involved with discontinuing a student from such a critical and exciting experience as student teaching will find the process painful. The decision must be made with the assurance that many public school students will benefit from the decision. And so may the student teacher . . . in the long run.

❖ 5 ❖

Effective Public
Relations With Schools

JOY MILLAR

The role of the local school district is paramount in the educational process of the student teacher. Therefore, the university's ability to successfully involve the public schools in this field experience is of great importance. A relationship of trust and cooperation doesn't happen overnight, or without a very conscientious effort by the university to create an avenue of communication and a feeling of mutual respect. Therefore, the university's student teacher program coordinator is in the key position to establish and foster the effective relations with the local schools that are vital to the success of the university's field experience for their student teachers. He or she must not only have an organized approach to the process of placing the student teachers but must also be willing to respond quickly to any problem that arises during the semester and have the capability of effecting an appropriate remedy.

Indeed, public relations is a vital and ongoing concern of the program coordinator. The process of finding suitable placements for the student teachers in the local public schools is the task that provides the vehicle for establishing a positive relationship between the university and the local school district. One such process covers a period of 4 months and begins with an interview of the student teacher by the student teacher program coordinator. This interview is informal but very important to both people involved. This 15- or 20-minute visit gives the student an opportunity to tell the program coordinator about placement preferences, and the coordinator gleans details about the student that help to match him or her with the best possible cooperating teacher.

It is best for placement purposes to have an interview form to follow and complete on each student. The interview provides the opportunity to establish a positive rapport with the student as well as providing the program coordinator some basic information about the student's communication ability. The information needed begins with the student's phone number and address. Note the field (elementary or secondary), degree (post or undergraduate), emphasis, and minor. It is helpful to have the students talk about their general background. Questions about their hometown; travel experiences; hobbies, interests, and accomplishments; and family all help you get a handle on the kind of life experiences they will bring to the classroom. Another area of information that is very relevant is the nature and extent of any previous teaching experiences they have had. What have they done in their past that tells them that they want to be teachers? Have they taught Sunday school, babysat, worked in summer camps, substituted in classrooms, or tutored children? If their experiences with young people are limited to what has been required by college course work, then you certainly need to be aware of this. Not only will the prospective cooperating teacher appreciate knowing their degree of experience, but the kind of cooperating teacher needed for a novice student teacher, as compared to one who has been doing substituting for 5 years, is obvious.

If the students are familiar with the local schools and can tell you who they want to be placed with, it is a simple matter of making a note of this. However, if they are unaware of any specific persons with whom they might request placement, then questions must be asked concerning the type of cooperating teacher with whom they would like to be placed. Allow them the opportunity to describe their ideal teacher. Also ask them to share their description of the kind of classroom in which they would feel most comfortable. You will use this information when you go to the schools and meet with the school liaison, who is the public school faculty member chosen by the principal to coordinate the student teacher program with the university program coordinator. By the time you have finished this part of the interview, you should have a first and second choice of schools, the grade level preferred, and teachers' names. If transportation is going to be a problem, be sure to make note of this during the interview. With luck, there are schools within walking distance of the university.

The interview may be concluded with the old show biz line: "Don't call me, I'll call you," implying that from this point forward the program coordinator is in charge of making the placement arrangements, and when they are completed, the students will be promptly notified. Assure them that you will be busy working on the placement they want, but that it will be 2 or 3 months before they can expect a call about their placement possibility. The time frame depends on whether it is a fall or spring semester placement. For a spring placement, the time is less. Interviews are in September and notices are usually given by late October or early November, because students need to know their placement before the Christmas break. If it is a fall placement, the waiting period is longer. School officials like to wait until after their spring break to start looking at fall considerations, and it is certainly important to honor this time factor. Never miss an opportunity to demonstrate an awareness of and willingness to comply with the procedures of the local school district. Obviously, the public school faculty is not in place as it is in September, when the spring placements are being made. This makes the process more time-consuming. Therefore, the waiting period for the fall student teacher is longer by almost a month.

With secondary student teachers, it is very helpful to contact their departments for any information that will help you make the best possible placement for them. Usually, there is an individual in each department who is responsible for the supervision of student teachers. Sometimes, however, a committee screens and provides dialogue concerning the placement of a secondary student. The secondary departments in the public schools often have close working relationships with their various university counterparts, and they may suggest teachers with whom the student teacher would do best. It is the role of the student teacher program coordinator to initiate communication between the education college and the many university colleges that are preparing students to be educators. This communication is critical to the success of a consistent and well-articulated field experience program at any university.

The next major step in this placement process is for the student teacher coordinator to meet with the individual school liaisons. Plan to meet on their campus for at least 1 hour. Going to their school is another way to signal your respect and appreciation for their involvement with the university's student teaching program. Many times this will give you the opportunity to exchange greetings with the principal or meet other faculty in the course of deciding placements. Make the appointments at least 2 weeks in advance, because the liaison needs time to prepare. It is the liaison's responsibility to present to the principal for administrative approval the names of the teachers who have indicated that they want to have a student teacher. Consequently, at the coordinator/liaison meeting, only faculty who have been approved by their principal to have a student teacher are considered.

The goal of the university program coordinator/public school liaison meeting is to make the best possible match between the student teacher and the public school faculty member. At this time, the program coordinator's knowledge about the needs of the student teacher are shared with the liaison. In turn, the liaison (who is in a position to know the potential cooperating teachers) can make an educated determination as to who will work best with whom. The student teacher's personal data sheet (PDS) is left with the liaison. This PDS is part of the student teacher application, and it begins with information about educational background. The following details are asked: all colleges attended, summary of experience working with children, scholastic or other honors received in high school or college, extracurricular activities, and list of courses and credit hours in both major and minor fields.

In addition to academic information, there are questions that reflect upon the student's philosophy about becoming a teacher. Why do you want to be a teacher? What qualities do you believe make a good teacher? Why do you want to student teach in the district for which you have applied? What do you see yourself doing over the next several years to improve your abilities as a professional teacher? What are your hobbies or personal interests? What is your personal philosophy of education?

The best possible scenario for the student teacher coordinator is to have more faculty members wanting a student teacher than there are requests for faculty. If this is the case, the university program coordinator takes a copy of those teachers who have requested a student teacher and have been cleared by the administration for possible future student teaching placements. This placing of student teachers isn't accomplished in one fell swoop. There will be stragglers in the process, for all sorts of reasons—life changes, completing course work, and so on. Being able to know which teachers at which schools want student teachers allows for a much more expeditious completion of the placement task.

Following the initial meeting between the student teacher coordinator and the public school liaison, the liaison gives the public school faculty member the student teacher's PDS as a kind of introduction to the student. If he or she is interested in interviewing the student, then this is communicated to the student teacher coordinator. The prospective student teacher is telephoned by the university coordinator and is given a 2-week period in which to call the teacher, arrange for an interview date, and complete the interview. The student teacher is impressed with the importance of correct protocol. Be prompt in calling the teacher, because this shows appreciation for the placement possibility and, naturally, their promptness reflects positively on the university as well as on the professional conduct of the student. Also, the classroom teacher's role is acknowledged as important, which has a positive impact upon the relationship between the university and the school. The interview visit should occur in the teacher's classroom, and the student teacher should approach this meeting as similar to a formal interview for a job. If, for whatever reason, the teacher is unwilling to take the student teacher, this is communicated to the liaison, who informs the university program coordinator. It is then the responsibility of the university program coordinator to seek a placement with the student teacher's second choice.

From the initial meeting between the university coordinator and the public school liaison, approximately 6 weeks elapse before contracts binding their professional commitment are ready for mutual agreement and signatures. During this time, recently cleared students wishing to student teach are dealt with, and original placements are changed. All of these negotiations and arrangements require several trips back to the schools for the university coordinator. These necessary travels really work to the advantage of the relationship between the public schools and the university. A brief chat here, working for a solution to a placement problem there; it all adds up to better communication and a feeling of camaraderie that is invaluable to the interaction between the two educational entities.

Finally, when negotiations are complete, contracts are placed in a large envelope and hand-delivered to the school liaison. Once again, this face-to-face contact is a timely public relations tool that improves upon mailing contracts to the schools. One week's time is given for the contracts to be signed by the school principal and the cooperating teacher. After they have been collected by the university coordinator, they are placed in the student teachers' application files; each student teacher receives a copy of his or her contract at a general meeting of all student teachers near the close of the semester. This is the final time that the student teachers are gathered on campus for instructions concerning their field experience.

Throughout the placement process and also when formulating the field experience program, good public relations is the key to a successful school year in which the university and the public schools work together for the benefit of both the schoolchildren and the university student teachers. An annual meeting of all the liaisons and the university supervisors at the university is an excellent way to begin the year. In late August, an informal get-together of university and public school persons should be provided. At this time, the supervisors and liaisons could be introduced and have the opportunity to discuss their plans for the coming semester. A review of the placement process should be presented, and any problems encountered by the university program coordinator the previous year are addressed. Questions about the supervision of the student teachers by the university, and any other topics of interest, are also on the agenda. This gathering gives the liaisons an opportunity to meet one another, to share some of their training sessions topics, and to discuss mutual problems or questions. Something good happens when all the players get together and share some time over cold drinks and cookies.

In addition, at the end of the school year in May or early June, the university student teacher program coordinator recognizes the importance of continuing good working relationships with the liaisons by mailing them personal thank-you notes for their efforts during the past two semesters. Gratitude expressed in writing not only says "thank you" but also sends the message that the university is aware of the importance of their role. Genuine appreciation, expressed on university stationery, is validation of the time and effort spent during the school year in working with the student teachers and their faculty.

It has been my experience that the key ingredient to the enhancement of effective public relations with the local public schools is conveying respect and appreciation, via personal contacts, for the teachers and administrators who involve themselves with the university field experience programs. Teachers especially respond positively to the university's need for their expertise. Showing respect and appreciation is the best way I know to get rid of the traditional "attitudes" that hinder a good rapport.

An example that demonstrates the importance of open communication and positive rapport is the suggestion from an elementary school liaison that the university have one supervisor assigned to a specific school, instead of more than one supervisor at each elementary school. That was the turning point in the university's relationship with that particular school. When this suggestion was acted upon, it not only created a continuity that had been missing in the program but also signaled (to a school that had been very vocal in its criticism of the university) that input from a local school could and did have an impact on the university's program. In fact, by the following semester, there were measurable positive effects of the newly established regime of one university supervisor per elementary school, where possible. Nothing mends fences like evidence of respect for ideas proposed by those affected and involved in the process, in this case, the classroom teachers. True, Rome wasn't built in a day, but when an openness to constructive criticism is demonstrated, effective relations between the public schools and institutions of higher learning are in progress.

6

Managing the Field Experience Office and Faculty

MARTHA M. MOBLEY

The acknowledged importance of practical experience with school students in the teacher preparation program of any college or university establishes the critical role played by the office responsible for field placement, coordination, and supervision. This office is—in a real sense—the visible, functional bridge between the public and private school teachers involved and the teacher preparation faculty of the college. An effective field office bridge enables prospective teachers to move between the two worlds, learning from one another and from those on whom they try their fledgling teaching skills.

The person responsible for the university field office plays a vital role as go-between ombudsman, which can be challenging and rewarding professionally; as with any position in the middle, the pitfalls, pressures, and problems can be daunting. Managing the office requires a wide range of skills and experience as well as a clear sense of mission. Everything from hand-holding and counseling through computerizing a systems approach to the information flow is involved. Even having all this and a clear vision of what *should be* isn't enough. There must be an understanding of the structure of both the school and the university, the players in each, and the games usually going on. Without the keen sensitivity to the power plays extant, the best intentioned theoretical field director will fall on hard times.

To begin, the management functions of planning, organizing, motivating, and communicating bear examination.

Planning

Of the basic functions designed to provide focus and direction to the field experience office, planning is most fundamental. Establishing office goals and evaluating specific, preferably measurable, objectives leading to the accomplishment of the goals are at the heart of this aspect of management. It includes forecasting events, anticipating problems, and determining actions to meet these and other exigencies as they arise.

One tool useful for planning events in the field experience office is an annual calendar of activities. One example follows:

Office of Field Experience
CALENDAR OF ACTIVITIES
January/August

1. Conduct orientation for outgoing student teachers.
2. Assign student teachers and junior field participants to college-based supervisors.
3. Prepare information packets for field-based supervisors of student teachers and field experience students.
4. Finalize and print agenda and other materials for meeting with faculty and administrators and college-based supervisors.
5. Schedule meetings with college-based and field-based supervisors.

6. Invite adjunct instructors of courses requiring a field-based experience to meet and review university policies, practices, and procedures.
7. Schedule meetings with Field Experience Advisory Committee.
8. Prepare, distribute, and post invitation to Student Teacher Application seminars.
9. Prepare, distribute, and post announcements of orientation meetings for pre-student teaching field-based experience.
10. Update/revise Student Teaching Calendar for following semester. Calendar to be distributed at Orientation Seminars for outgoing student teachers.

February/September

1. Prepare payment requests for college-based supervisors of student teachers.
2. Conduct orientation sessions for pre-student teaching field-based experience.
3. Finalize and distribute semester calendar for field-based experience students.
4. Conduct Student Teacher Application seminars.
5. Announce the deadlines for student teaching applications in campus newsletters and newspapers.
6. Place pre-student teaching field experience students.

March/October

1. Review student teaching applications for next semester.
2. Interview each applicant for student teaching.
3. Notify students regarding the status of their files, identifying missing items or completeness of file.
4. Create a computer file for each student teaching applicant as well as a Pendaflex file. Information maintained and retrievable by discipline: early childhood, English, special education, and so on; graduate or undergraduate status; year of graduation, and so on.

5. Assign and notify each student teacher of his/her placement(s) by 15th of month.

6. Conduct meetings for supervisors, college-based and field-based, and advisory committee.

7. Begin preparation for end-of-year recognition of field-based supervisors.

8. Recognize building administrators and field-based supervisors for their roles in the development of future teachers.

9. Generate and distribute statistical reports for field experience students for semester. Include (a) total number of students placed; (b) number of students by discipline; (c) placements by districts/schools; (d) placement by supervisors; and (e) comparison of number of placements with previous semester/year.

April/November

1. Prepare certificates (incentives) for field-based supervisors.

2. Conduct meetings for supervisors, college-based and field-based, and advisory committee.

3. Provide department chairs with statistical information regarding number of student teaching applications received for following semester by status of students (graduate/undergraduate) and area(s) of certification.

4. Request from faculty and college-based supervisors suggestions for future placements of student teachers and field experience students.

5. Identify current student teachers to address orientation seminar for next semester's student teachers.

6. Prepare budget request for following year.

May/December

1. File completed student teaching evaluations from college-based and field-based supervisors.

2. Review each individual student teacher's file for completeness before recommending him or her for certification.

3. Return completed student teaching files to departments of origin.

4. Download to disc information regarding graduating students.

5. Update computer files for names, addresses, and dates of student teaching placement, including name of district, building, grade level(s), and cooperating teacher(s).

6. Prepare and submit mileage reimbursement for college-based supervisors of student teachers and participant/observers.

7. Finalize student teacher placements for following semester.

8. Hold recognition event for field-based supervisors.

9. Arrange pre-student teaching field experiences for Summer Sessions I and II.

10. Conduct final meeting with college-based supervisors, field-based supervisors, and advisory committee.

June/July

1. Complete annual report for office of field placement.

2. Update, revise *Guide for Student Teaching* and *Guide for Pre-Student Teaching Field Experience*.

3. Revise application forms, guidelines, and so on.

4. Prepare thank-you letters to district administrators and field-based supervisors.

5. Finalize field experience calendars for following semester.

6. Invite a panel of student teachers to present at Orientation to Student Teaching.

7. Provide college-based supervisors with names, addresses, and so on of students for whom they will be responsible.

While offering a flexible approach to events and time management, this calendar recognizes the placement cycle as well as the academic calendar. Tasks may be established by month or priority in order to provide information for semester and annual calendars to be distributed to students, supervisors, and administrators.

The forecasting of events and selecting of courses of appropriate actions is largely based upon past assumptions and experience. Beyond the calendar, a field experience office may use a written practice statement for a change of placement for field experience students. The following practice statement was developed in concert by faculty, supervisors, and university administrators.

Practice Statement: Change of Placement

There may be an occasion during the student teaching or field placement semester when a change of assignment should be considered. The request of change of placement may be initiated on a case by case basis.

1. On recommendation of college-based supervisor
2. On request of field-based supervisor, school administrator, or district contact person
3. On request of student teacher

For placement change to be made:

A. College-based supervisor to visit classroom to discuss the request with student teacher before placement change is made. Alternative methods of resolving problem to be discussed during this visit.
B. College-based supervisor to be informed of request if he or she is not the initiator. Classroom visit to be initiated as described in "A."
C. Director of field placement is to be informed of request and progress of negotiations.
D. College-based supervisor to discuss the request to move student with field-based supervisor, school administrator, and director of field placement before final decision is reached. Decision to be made based on input of major players.
E. District contact person to be kept informed on possibility for change.

    F. If situation cannot be resolved, change to be made by office of field experience.

Change of Assignment Priorities for Field Placement/Student Teaching:

1. Replacement secured in a different school and district.
2. Replacement to be considered in another school within the district.

Organizing

    Organizing the field experience office entails generating daily lists, letters, forms, faxes, and telephone calls, as well as visits from students, supervisors, faculty members, administrators, parents, and staff. The ability to establish the flow of information and people so that all members of the field office staff understand it is among the highest priorities in a smoothly functioning and flexibly responsive field experience office.

    The field office manages placements in a series of progressively complex, planned experiences in K-12 schools. With a foot in each camp, the staff must be able to recognize and respond to student needs of public schools as well as those of the university. Organizing a policy/procedure/practice manual may be a priority consideration. An office manual might be a simple hole-punched looseleaf, emphasizing what has worked, when, and how. Or it may be a more sophisticated manual containing policies by number and sequence, revised annually. It provides a definite, clear point of reference while reducing personal and staff stress.

    The process of organizing the office functions involves identifying specific procedures and activities as well as the resources available to accomplish them. Among these essential resources a field director will want to consider are personal computers, financial support, and using advisory and faculty committees.

Personnel

Field office staff are people dealing with people with feelings of anxiety, resistance, or excitement. Each employee needs to know what's important to individual students, faculty members, or parents—any person who walks through the office door—in order to both respond with empathy and influence the service so that services and needs can be more closely aligned.

Because satisfying the customer is always the best operating philosophy, it isn't hard to arrive at the understanding that people want their problems—small or complex, real or imagined—to be solved quickly and treated personally with dignity and respect. Students particularly have the right to expect staff members to respond with appropriate information while looking at the situation from the student's perspective. Information should be available, convenient, reliable, and tailored to their needs.

The challenge to the field service director is to deliberately select and hire employees who want close contact and interaction with many people, willingly using an unbureaucratic approach. It means trusting and training people; giving them opportunities to involve themselves more freely in the workplace; and tapping their knowledge, skills, and commitment. It means instilling a loyalty to the office and its functions while providing quality service. A caring and committed director will share knowledge, expertise, and resources with people who believe, as he or she does, that the field office exists not only to help but also to ensure that technical assistance and training are available to people who effect the program as a means to develop and promote them. But to learn what is effective for themselves and the organization, individuals also need coaching, mentoring, and direct and clear feedback about performance and styles. Blessed be the risk-takers and innovators, for they will be recognized and rewarded for wanting to make changes while caring about others.

Computers

Second only to the people who staff the field office are computers to manage the extensive data. To function successfully, the data generated must be condensed into manageable dimensions. This process is started at the moment a prospective student submits an application. Part of the application is a preprinted Rolodex control card, on which is requested such basic information as name, address, telephone number, Social Security number, student status, and major. Entered into the database, this information is the foundation for each student's file to which additional information is added as the student advances through the field experience components. Computer files collect, record, and store names, addresses, grade levels of the supervisors and administrators. Dates of submitted evaluations are added, as are those indicating that thank-you letters and incentives were sent. Labels, letters, certificates, and reports can be computer-generated, as can lists of potential graduate students. Improved public relations, visibility, and, certainly, greater cooperation with the school personnel are possible.

Several databases adapt successfully for use within field experience offices to manage the enormous, continuous flow of information. *Paradox with Windows* keeps track of vast amounts of knowledge, which of course is what computers do well. *Q & A* does a creditable job of list-making and retrieval of basic information. Either program, coupled with a word-processing package such as *WordPerfect* or *WordStar*, is able to control the flow of office information about student placements and supervisor assignments with accuracy and speed, qualities that are essential to a smoothly functioning program.

Budget

Organizing is more than the process of identifying and grouping work to be done; it must also establish the relationships between work and resources. Assisting people—prospective teachers and those working with them—is the first and highest priority of the field office. This demands quality personnel, computers, and other technological aids. Money and budget are the organizing task of the office manager, for the piper must be paid.

The costs of staff time, printing, computers, and mailing are a reality and must be planned and accounted for. Included in the activities and functions of the experience office are:

— Staff salaries and fringe benefits
— Advisory committees' expenses
— Contract service/repair of equipment
— Equipment (e.g., computers, mailing devices, fax machines, etc.)
— Incentives for cooperating teachers, schools, and districts
— In-service programs (e.g., staff retreats and seminars)
— Meals, refreshments
— Postage and printing
— Speaker fees
— Telephone and fax
— Travel reimbursement
— Training for improved staff performance

Annual budgetary requests based on past experience and future plans must stay within university set guidelines and should match the projected objectives.

Advisory Committee

One of the problems confronting a field director is that of university staff who have spent limited time in the schools of 1994 and their sense of shareability. A forum, such as an advisory committee, provides a time and place for the public school and the college to come together. One reality is that student teachers in public and private colleges and universities are products of the public schools.

Field experience directors often are called upon to manage controversial and sensitive aspects of teacher education. Among the current topics are child abuse, AIDS, multiculturalism, computer education, and any subject that concerns faculty or administrators as they affect the development of prospective teachers. Inclusion of interested and involved parties in all phases of the design, implementation, and evaluation of field placement procedures is vital to generate support, especially on emotional and delicate issues.

An advisory committee is one appropriate avenue to develop support and engender commitment to the clinical aspects of teacher preparation. Ideally, membership should include university faculty representing all the colleges engaged in teacher preparation, current student and program graduates, district and school administrators, and cooperating teachers. The purpose of an advisory committee is to support the goals of the office. This process also may help the field experience office to make proactive decisions, with a design to:

— Providing visible approval or sanction;
— Involving the major supporters in the process;
— Setting the program direction by offering the goals, objectives, and methods;
— Providing support and continuity for the program;
— Providing a forum for problem solving that might arise in field settings; and
— Reinforcing the global nature of field experience, in that individuals are encouraged to have a vested interest in simultaneously improving the education of university students and students within the K-12 schools.

Meeting at regularly scheduled intervals with a focused agenda, strong, articulate committee members communicate the realities of field experience so that each prospective teacher gains and, ultimately, the entire profession will benefit.

Motivating

A good field experience office depends on enthusiasm, initiative, cooperation, and the desire of the total staff to achieve the goals of sound preservice teacher education. Theories of motivation consistently express a central concept: An individual's motivational drive can be explained in terms of satisfying personal needs.

Most staff members are better motivated when they see and understand clear-cut goals and objectives. Regular meetings with supervisors and staff members help to inform everyone about issues, reactions, and changes. On the job, people will want to apply themselves better and more diligently to solve problems and get the job done. These are the people who provide the service, guide the students, and connect the university and the public schools.

Unless training and development are appropriate and ongoing, good planning and organizing alone will not guarantee that the desired performance of the office staff will take place. Both are avenues that may encourage staff members to improve performance so that they can gain greater expertise in their current jobs and become eligible for promotion. Retreats, seminars, and ongoing training demonstrate the university's commitment to its employees and their value. A special day or two away from the office is a treat and builds esprit de corps if properly developed.

One problem historically plaguing field office directors and the office is that of their placement in the college structure. A field experience office may be appended to one or more departments, and its director may be lacking faculty status and rank. Its unimportance on the college organizational charts communicates a resistance to field courses and their supervision, detailing this work to hired adjuncts. Most tenure committees neither acknowledge nor reward faculty members for field assignments, further denigrating the centrality of this work for faculty promotion and teacher preparation.

Typically field offices are run hat-in-hand, with directors creatively seeking resources and funding. What seems obvious for improved status is the need for strong and supportive voices and reassuring resources from the education deans and the professional unions, communicating their belief in and commitment to school-based field experience.

Communicating

Communicating effectively with students, supervisors, district personnel, university faculty, advisory committee members, administrators, and others is an absolute necessity. Relationships are key to the success of the field office. In a real sense, it is a three-ring circus. It is more than sending and receiving information; it is the means by which attitudes and behaviors are changed.

Several low-cost approaches include easily recognized logos on stationery, information packets, and posters. Specific colors designating specific semesters also can ensure greater success. Consider the many pieces of paper that pass through the office in a semester, and hole-punch or staple them into binders, labeled for instant identification and immediate retrieval.

A monthly newsletter or a column in the school of education newsletter can also help. Initiatives, cluster placements, unusual activities, or programs that highlight students and schools can be news items. Even a single-page newsletter that also is a self-mailer can be effective.

Videotaping, perhaps for performance assessment of students or expanding instructional strategies for the university classroom, is also a highly effective method of communicating. Some state departments of education, as well as schools of education, insist that a videotaped segment of a teacher instructing an actual classroom be submitted as preliminary to state certification.

Although not new to the world of education, many office personnel may have limited experience working videotaping equipment. Small successful experiments have been conducted where pairs of student teachers videotaped each other and also jointly analyzed each other's performance.

For faculty members, professional reading helps; seminars also help. But in the long run, if universities and public schools are to communicate, cooperation and collaboration on a constant basis between and among professionals remain fundamental. Interactive seminars, at the university and at school sites, focused on reflective teaching strategies or on culturally sensitive issues are extremely useful, particularly when coupled with on-site observation and teaching experiences. The regular appearance of college faculty at public schools, offering courses and insight and conducting research, speaks to the everlasting interdependence between the schools and the colleges of education.

More than factual information is communicated in most instances. Attitudes are communicated. Respect is communicated. Feelings are transmitted. The message of "people first" emanating from the field experience office is the most desired communication of all.

Field experience programs are messy. Things do not always go as planned. People are not always happy. Situations are not perfect.

Teacher education is a task of both the university and the school district. Implicit in this vision is that a joint effort between the two institutions will prepare more effective teachers who, in turn, will improve the teaching and learning of all children. Explicitly, the field office's responsibility is to generate linkages between theory and practice. Keeping to the task of seeing that the enterprise is focused on this mission, and not the convenience and comfort of the college faculty or the schools' administration, is the challenge to the director.

It shall be the director's responsibility to remind faculty, student teachers, cooperating staff, and supervisors of this goal, and to have the power to persuade those who do not conform to its spirit and substance, with the backing of the faculty governing body and deans so that the quality of each student's field experience is maximized.

Recommended Reading

Bolmar, L. G., & Deal, T. E. (1984). *Modern approaches to understanding and managing organizations*. San Francisco: Jossey-Bass.

Covey, S. R. (1991). *Principle-centered leadership*. New York: Summit.

Hale, S. J., & Williams, M. W. (1989). *Managing change: A guide to producing innovation from within*. Washington, DC: The Urban Institute Press.

Mobley, M. M. (1993, April 28). *Videotaping: Technology for student teaching feedback*. Paper presented at New England Research Organization, Portsmouth, NH.

Walters, D. M. (1984). *The management team*. Glendora, CA: Royal Cassettes.

Yopp, H. K., Guillaume, A. M., & Savage, T. V. (1993-94). Collaboration at the grassroots: Implementing the professional development school concept. *Action in Teacher Education, 15*(4), 29-35.

Postbaccalaureate Field Experiences

DALE L. LANGE

Introduction and Context

In the 1990s teacher education programs face a lack of both general confidence and resources in the development of teachers for initial licensure. To combat this attitude and this reality, such programs utilize a variety of strategies to restructure or reorient their responsibilities for the preparation of beginning teachers. Some of the strategies involve the use of outcome-based teacher education, the creation of a variety of partnerships with schools, collaborations of school and university in professional development and professional practice schools, internships, and residen-

AUTHOR'S NOTE: Some of the language and ideas presented here originally appeared in Lange (1990). © 1990 by Cambridge University Press. Reprinted with permission of Cambridge University Press.

cies, as well as complete program redesign that might consist of many of these strategies. One such program redesign includes postbaccalaureate teacher development. The example employed in this chapter to exemplify the principles of clinical experiences within postbaccalaureate initial teacher development is that of the University of Minnesota.

Because of impending major budget reductions to the College of Education at the University of Minnesota in the mid-1980s, the faculty participated in the redesign of its initial teacher development program, changing it over time from undergraduate to postbaccalaureate. That change began in 1987, when implementation started, and will be finished in 1995, when all programs will be postbaccalaureate. This change generated very laudatory comments from university faculty and school administrators; however, it only put off major budget reductions until 1992, when the college had finished the conversion of only two thirds of its programs.

Now that the context has been described briefly, what are the principles upon which a postbaccalaureate program, including clinical experiences, is established? What does that program look like? How has it worked? Answers to these questions are the content of this chapter.

A Framework for Teacher Development

Many influences have called for change in the structuring and direction of teacher development programs (e.g., Carnegie Forum, 1986; Goodlad, 1990; The Holmes Group, 1986). The latest complete thinking on the development of teachers relates not just to postbaccalaureate teacher education but also to a stream of continuing preparation for the teaching profession that begins with the recruitment of individuals to teacher education and follows them through a B.A./B.S. degree, seminars and internships through a 5th year in a B.Ped. or B.Ed., to licensing, and finally to continuing professional development (Goodlad, 1994), continuing licensure (Minnesota Board of Teaching, 1994), and advanced voluntary, national licensure (National Board for Professional Teaching Standards, 1991). As a result, postbaccalaureate teacher education programs must not be seen as a panacea, but within a larger framework of work by an engaged profession of teacher educators who are grappling with 'the many, continuing policy issues that abound in the development of a profession.

Within its own policy context, the University of Minnesota's College of Education postbaccalaureate teacher development program functions within the general framework and principles presented by Mulkeen and Tetenbaum (1987; Tetenbaum & Mulkeen, 1986), a framework that allows development from preservice, graduate, and development of career ladder skills, to open-ended continuing professional development. In their two articles, Mulkeen and Tetenbaum present six very broad characteristics of the future technological society, from which implications are drawn for teacher education and a nine-feature model of teacher development is supported. From these core features, there is a postbaccalaureate program developed, in which clinical experiences are discussed.

Characteristics

1. *The 21st century will be knowledge-based.* Social problems will be highly complex (hunger, overpopulation, needs for and supply of energy, urban decay, etc.). Thus the issue for society as a whole must be how to organize to make wise, informed, and intelligent decisions.

2. *The 21st century will see an increase information flow.* Scientific and technical knowledge doubles every 5.5 years. An overview of the contribution of research in instructional methods and contributions to classroom learning (Walberg, Schiller, & Haertel, 1979) relates positive results from more than 2,000 controlled studies; however, there are about 4,000 more that have not been considered.

3. *The 21st century will see rapid change and impermanence.* Individuals will never be able to complete their education; they will also not expect to enter a job or profession and remain in it without retraining.

4. *The 21st century will see an increase in decentralization of organizations, institutions, and systems.* Societal structures, from business and industry to religious institutions and schools, will experience decentralization of power, because problems are generally solved in groups of people who collaborate and share expertise and perspectives.

5. *The 21st century will be people-oriented.* People are the nation's most important asset. Individuals' need for self-determination and input into the decision-making processes that affect them are important for the cultivation of experimentation, innovation, and individual entrepreneurship in our culture.

6. *The 21st century will see major demographic shifts.* This condition is particularly true for the United States ethnic and racial composition. The single largest, fastest-growing minority population in this country is Hispanic in origin. Differential birthrates suggest that the United States will see more blacks, fewer whites, as many Hispanics as blacks, and more Asians.

Implications

1. The teaching profession must attract some of the "best and brightest," especially persons of color.
2. Teachers will have to become facilitators, not repositories of knowledge. They will need preparation in a variety of alternatives in pedagogy and curriculum development (Schubert, 1986).
3. Lifelong learning must be a construct in every teacher development program.
4. Experimentation, risk-taking, autonomy, and flexibility must be key elements in the development of a model of schooling and teacher development that places responsibility for learning on students, giving them freedom to try, test, innovate, and create.

5. Schools and teacher development programs must prepare teachers to take responsibility for professional decisions that affect the classroom.

6. Teacher development programs must actively orient the development of teachers toward pedagogy and curriculum that respond to the evolving nature of our multicultural society.

A Model and Its Core Features

From these characteristics and implications, the Tetenbaum and Mulkeen (1986) model includes nine core features.

1. Field-Based. Preservice teacher development takes place on-site, in schools, in cooperation with collegiate teacher development programs. Professional development or practice schools serve this purpose.

2. Problem-Centered. Curriculum and instructional practice in teacher development are organized around the resolution of identified problems in actual classes, in real schools.

3. Technology-Driven. Computers, videotape, videodisc, satellite hookups, and E-mail are key components in a problem-resolving mode of instruction.

4. Experimental Sharing. Collegiate, school, supervisory, and professional staff share with the developing teacher(s) in the identification and organization of resolutions to curricular and instructional problems.

5. Developmental. The teacher development program meets the needs of increasingly sophisticated and multicultural professionals.

6. Competency-Based. While focusing on the resolution of curricular and instructional problems, the teacher development program is oriented toward knowledge, skills, and attitudes that are appropriate to each experiential level identified, taught, practiced, and evaluated.

7. *Expertly Staffed.* Problem resolution comes about because of a constellation of staff who work together: school staff, university faculty, representatives of community agencies, consultants from the community, and the like.

8. *Critical Mass.* A concentration of professional staff within a school setting, using risk-taking and experimentation, makes the process of problem resolution possible.

9. *Open-Ended.* The model is open-ended, suggesting that professional development is never-ending and lifelong.

The Resulting Postbaccalaureate
Teacher Development Program

The application of a model is always problematic because of the compromises that are made between the theoretical principles and the reality of the situation. Much has been accomplished since the initialization of the program in the 1987-1988 academic year when two programs, Social Studies and Second Language and Cultures Education, risked the establishment of the program within the framework. The details are being filled in; the model and its implications serve as a strong guide to the now unified program.

In the postbaccalaureate program at the University of Minnesota, students are admitted to a Master of Education degree by licensure area. The completion of the licensure program and the Master of Education degree are not coterminous, the latter being completed after 1 year of teaching experience. In cohorts, approximately 30 students are admitted to 14 licensure areas each year. On the average, these students are approximately 30 years old, with GPAs in the range of 3.2 to 3.5, depending on licensure area. In other words, they are experienced, intelligent, and capable. They have goals in mind, want to be teachers, and are driven to finish in the 12 to 15 months allotted to the program for initial licensure.

In its simplest description, the program comprises three categories of competencies: (a) foundations of education (school and its relationship to society; interpersonal and personality effects on learning, including those of inclusion and diversity; classroom assessment; learning and cognitive functions of education; basic personal and community health, including drug education; and finally, physical and biological development); (b) licensure area content pedagogy (e.g., elementary education, physical sciences, French, and agriculture education); and (c) clinical experiences, largely in the hands of those professorial staff who work with content pedagogy. In its more complicated version, each content area develops clinical experiences to fit with its own needs.

Models are goals toward which programs aspire. This post-baccalaureate teacher development program is continuing to develop within this framework. Participants in the program are highly selected, with students of color being supported by College of Education funds mainly in a Multicultural Teacher Development Project (local recruitment) and the Common Ground Consortium (distance recruitment with nine historical black colleges and universities). The St. Paul-based Bush Foundation has been supportive of the latter program. A common foundations program has been constructed for all participants in what is being considered a unified program; nine common outcomes have been established; means of evaluating the outcomes are being piloted; a common knowledge base, supported by the problematic of reflective teaching, has been adopted and is being implemented; and some common research themes across licensure areas have been initially explored and reported on. Clinical experiences have a broader field base than in the limited 10 weeks of student teaching of the former undergraduate teacher preparation program, involving more local staff and schools. The program is considered open-ended and developmental because the Master of Education is finished in the year(s) after initial licensure has been obtained.

Clinical or Field Experiences Within a Postbaccalaureate Teacher Development Program

General Description

Clinical or field experiences in this postbaccalaureate teacher development program take place over the 9 months of the academic year while schools are in session. Such is the case because students in the program are only working toward licensure. Focus on their preparation for teaching is their only concern. As a result, three phases of clinical experiences have evolved: (a) awareness, (b) practice, and (c) induction. Each phase has its own set of activities and content, and the phases take place in different settings: an elementary education center where more than one postbaccalaureate student works with a school released supervisor and a university supervisor; a professional development school where both university and school faculty work collaboratively to prepare teachers and work on each other's needs; in a practicum placement where only some aspects of the clinical experiences program are offered; in a series of placements specifically designed for the three levels in different school districts; in a school district where students are rotated among schools for different levels of the program; and in a content area where students are alternated among teachers for the different levels of clinical experiences. All of these permutations exist in some form or other.

Awareness Phase

Observation is the major activity in the first 3 months of this phase. Although much of the observation takes place internal to schools in the observation of student-to-teacher and teacher-to-student relationships, observation activities are accomplished externally as well, within the community. *External* kinds of activities have consisted of interviews and discussion with mayors in school communities, school board members, city council members, and other kinds of community leaders on the importance of education to the community and on perceptions of issues such as community support for education, importance of school sports, and school violence that affects the community. Postbaccalaureate students have been required to observe school board meetings and other community meetings related to education and report those observations to their peers in seminars for that purpose.

Internal observations have focused largely on the interactions of students and teachers with one another as teachers teach and students learn. What are these relationships? How do they both help and hinder learning? What do teachers do that facilitates learning? How do students receive that facilitation? When is learning hindered? Why is it hindered? Postbaccalaureate students observe in more than one curricular area to determine how teaching and learning in those areas might be different from in their own. Postbaccalaureate students are asked to shadow a student for a day (they must get permission from the student to do so), and they interview principals, counselors, secretaries, janitors, bus drivers, and other people who make the school run, in order to recognize that the school itself is a community where the contributions of people outside the classroom contribute to the work of the classroom. In both the external and internal observations, students in the postbaccalaureate programs are learning the culture of the school from the perspective of the community outside as well as from within.

Practice Phase

All phases overlap to some degree. This phase is most intensive during the months of January through June. It begins almost immediately in the fall and carries through the third phase, induction. In this phase, there are three basic activities: tutoring, leading small group activities, and microteaching with both peers and students in classrooms.

Tutoring is one of the first intensive, interactive contacts that postbaccalaureate students have with students in schools. The purpose of tutoring is to provide an opportunity for the teacher-in-preparation to be in a classroom, observe students, and work intensively with one or more students through the resolution of a particular problem in a classroom situation. Reflection on this experience, its nature, the interaction, and the outcome(s) gives this postbaccalaureate student a major occasion to consider teaching as a profession, in courses and seminars in the licensure area.

A second, more challenging clinical or field activity is leading of small-group activities. Here, again, for the first time, the post-baccalaureate student is involved in the management of a classroom environment, at least partially, under the supervision of a cooperating teacher. The management required is not only the management of students but also the management of both instructional and curricular planning. Questions that require reflection in this phase are: How does the work with the small group fit into the instructional plan for the particular lesson? How does that lesson fit into a broader unit structure? How is the work of the small group evaluated? How do I assess my own management of the personal, instructional, and curricular plan for the work of the small group? Here, diaries, short reflective papers, and discussions in courses and seminars bring about an initial understanding of the complexity of the teaching act and the art required to put the many elements together for successful student learning.

A third element of practice, microteaching, could be in an actual school classroom with students or in a peer group. The purpose of microteaching has been carefully described by Allen and Ryan (1969) and includes controlled practice in real or simulated situations, with focus on real elements of instruction that allow for feedback from a group, from an individual supervisor, or through a set of criteria that the postbaccalaureate students can apply to their own instruction in private, through the use of videotape. The advantages of microteaching in a school or with peers intimate that microteaching with peers allows for practice with a teaching/learning strategy or any element of instruction, with the comfort of colleagues to give feedback prior to actual use with a group of students in school, whereas microteaching in schools provides a much more realistic situation. In the postbaccalaureate program at the University of Minnesota, both situations are used in the initial preparation of teachers.

Induction Phase

This phase is the most intense in the spring of the academic year, although the process begins in the winter. Postbaccalaureate students are in schools full-time at this point. At this phase of clinical experiences, the student is responsible for both the curriculum and the instructional program for two long periods. The purpose for two opportunities for intensive teaching is to give the student teacher experience in planning for, teaching, and evaluating teaching over two occasions so that he or she can make adjustments and/or teach at more than one level at this point.

Having more than one opportunity to teach, developing teachers, with the aid of videotaped lessons and feedback from both the cooperating teacher and the university supervisor, learn to resolve the teaching and learning problems that they face. They learn to evaluate themselves, applying the strategies they have learned from activities in the awareness and practices phases of the clinical experiences program. Thus, this phase is similar to a standard student teaching situation, with the exception that there are at least two occasions to practice the responsibility of full commitment for the curriculum, the instruction, and the assessment of students.

Conclusion

Clinical or field experiences in postbaccalaureate programs require extensive planning and communication among faculty and school personnel. Working with teacher centers, professional development schools, and school districts to bring such an intensive program of experience to those preparing for an initial professional license rewards everyone in the program. Everyone learns from the others, with the potential for breaking barriers between elementary, secondary, and postsecondary education. Such a condition creates an atmosphere through clinical experiences that gives confidence to the initially licensed teacher. Such confidence has been exhibited by those who have finished the program of licensure at the University of Minnesota. In fact, principals have given direct feedback, indicating, for example: "We hired your graduate and found him/her to be the equivalent of a second-year teacher." That is one measure of success to suggest that the clinical experiences program is working. We will watch it evolve as the rest of the program matures.

References

Allen, D., & Ryan, K. (1969). *Microteaching*. Reading, MA: Addison-Wesley.

Carnegie Forum on Education and the Economy. (1986). *A nation prepared: Teachers for the 21st century*. New York: Carnegie Education Foundation.

Goodlad, J. I. (1990). *Teachers for our nation's schools*. San Francisco: Jossey-Bass.

Goodlad, J. I. (1994). *Educational renewal: Better teachers, better schools*. San Francisco: Jossey-Bass.

Holmes Group, The. (1986). *Tomorrow's schools: Principles for the design of professional development schools*. East Lansing, MI: Author.

Lange, D. L. (1990). A blueprint for a teacher development program. In J. C. Richards & D. Nunan (Eds.), *Second language teacher education* (pp. 245-268). New York: Cambridge University Press.

Minnesota Board of Teaching. (1994). *Proposal for licensing system for Minnesota teachers* (Draft 2). St. Paul: Author.

Mulkeen, T. A., & Tetenbaum, T. J. (1987, Winter). An integrative model of teacher education and professional development. *Educational Horizons*, 85-87.

National Board for Professional Teaching Standards. (1991). *Toward high and rigorous standards for the teaching profession: Initial policies and perspectives of the National Board for Professional Teaching Standards* (3rd ed.). Detroit: Author.

Schubert, W. H. (1986). *Curriculum: Perspective, paradigm, and possibility*. New York: Macmillan.

Tetenbaum, T. J., & Mulkeen, T. A. (1986). Designing teacher education for the twenty-first century. *Journal of Higher Education, 57*, 621-636.

Walberg, H. J., Schiller, D., & Haertel, G. D. (1979). The quiet revolution in educational research. *Phi Delta Kappan, 61*, 179-183.

❖ 8 ❖

State Department Requirements
for Student Teaching

BEVERLY J. IRBY
GENEVIEVE BROWN

In today's mobile society, students seeking initial certification and credit for student teaching may be likely to move from state to state. Because requirements vary throughout the country, and because some states such as Alaska leave specific program requirements to the discretion of the universities, we advise that the student contact the specific university of choice within the state to determine guidelines for entering the student teaching program. It is important to remember that elementary and secondary student teaching requirements will differ; therefore, the student should indicate the student teaching grade level(s) and subject(s) for which he or she is applying.

Because space constraints prohibit giving detailed information regarding state department requirements for student teaching in all 50 states, this chapter offers representative examples (Andrews & Andrews, 1994). It is hoped that these selected cases will not only provide insights into the diverse guidelines that exist among the states but also prompt further investigation as needed. The following seven questions are frequently asked by students who are considering moving to another state to student teach.

Question 1: Do I have the professional education
requirements for student teaching in the particular state?

The following professional education coursework is most commonly required prior to student teaching; the states listed are exceptions (Table 8.1). Some states, such as Alabama, incorporate course content requirements within the approved program, rather than specifying particular courses.

Some states require other specific coursework, such as foundations or history of American education, school organization and planning, curriculum development, teacher reflection/research, cultural diversity, and/or instructional technology.

Question 2: Must I have field
experience prior to my student teaching?

The type and duration of field experience required prior to student teaching varies among the states. However, 37 of the states require some field experience prior to student teaching. Depending upon the state, duration of initial field experience may range from 40 hours to 300 hours. Some states, such as Delaware, require a specified number of clock hours of observation with each methods course. Field experiences in other states, such as Alabama, are an integral part of all professional courses.

Question 3: Do I have the required number
of subject matter courses for my teaching field?

Subject matter requirements for teaching fields in elementary, middle/junior high, secondary, and all levels vary greatly throughout the country. At the elementary level, 37 of the 50 states require

TABLE 8.1 Commonly Required Professional Education
            Coursework

Elementary Coursework	States That Are Exceptions
Social Foundations	Arizona, Connecticut, Illinois, Maine, Maryland, Massachusetts, Mississippi, Montana, Nebraska, New York, South Dakota, Vermont
Philosophy of Education	Arizona, Connecticut, Delaware, Illinois, Iowa, Maine, Maryland, Massachusetts, Mississippi, Montana, Nebraska, New York, Vermont, Washington
Human Growth and Development	Alaska, Arizona, Maine, Montana, Nebraska, Tennessee, Vermont
Instruction Strategies	Arizona, Delaware, Louisiana, Maine, Maryland, Montana, Nebraska, Nevada, Tennessee, Vermont, Virginia
Elementary Teaching Methods	Louisiana, Nebraska, New Jersey, Vermont
Reading Methods	New Jersey, Utah, Vermont

Secondary Coursework	States That Are Exceptions
Social Foundations	Connecticut, Delaware, Illinois, Iowa, Kentucky, Maine, Maryland, Massachusetts, Mississippi, Montana, Nevada, New York, South Dakota, Vermont, Virginia
Philosophy of Education	Arizona, Connecticut, Delaware, Georgia, Kentucky, Maine, Maryland, Massachusetts, Mississippi, Montana, Nevada, New Jersey, New York, Vermont, Washington
Human Growth and Development	Kentucky, Maine, Montana, Nevada, Tennessee, Vermont
Teaching Strategies	Arizona, Kentucky, Louisiana, Maine, Maryland, Montana, Nebraska, Nevada, Tennessee, Vermont, Virginia
Secondary Methods of Teaching	Kentucky, Louisiana, Massachusetts, Montana, Nevada, New Jersey, Vermont, Virginia, West Virginia

specific subject matter in a teaching field. For example, Wisconsin and Montana require a major and a minor, and Arizona requires 18 semester hours in a content area. Five of the states require a major in order to teach at the middle school or junior high level, and four (Alaska, Minnesota, North Dakota, and Wisconsin) require a major and a minor.

Vermont is the only state that does not have specific subject matter requirements for teaching at the secondary level. Ten states (Alaska, Arkansas, Idaho, Indiana, Kentucky, Michigan, South Dakota, Texas, Utah, and Wisconsin) require a major or a minor in a subject area. Twenty-nine states have minimum hours established in the subject area; 24 states specify components, rather than subject areas, that must be included in university programs.

*Question 4: Is my GPA adequate
to student teach in another state?*

Most universities require a minimum GPA for admission to the teacher education program and to student teaching, and in many cases GPA standards are set by the individual institution. Several states, such as Colorado, Florida, Kansas, and New Jersey, have a state requirement of a 2.5 GPA for initial teacher certification.

*Question 5: What are specific
requirements for the student teaching experience?*

Once again, specific requirements vary markedly from state to state. For example, 12 of the 50 states require that students teach in a multicultural setting; 9 require student teaching experiences with more than one group of students; and 11 states require student teaching experiences that include exceptional students. In addition, the time requirements for student teaching experiences differ. West Virginia, Wyoming, and Missouri do not mandate a designated amount of time to be spent in the student teaching experience; New Mexico specifies 180 contact hours; and California and Utah require one full semester. The number of weeks required ranges from 8 to 18.

Question 6: How will I be evaluated
during my student teaching experience?

All but 14 of the states stipulate that student teachers be evaluated on a specific set of requirements, which are generally established by the particular university. Eleven of the states require that a university supervisor and a cooperating teacher jointly evaluate the student teacher. New Hampshire, New Jersey, and Tennessee require that the principal of the school where the student teacher is located assume responsibility for evaluation. Fourteen states rely on the university supervisor to evaluate the student teacher, and 18 of the states utilize a combination of the university supervisor, the cooperating teacher, and the principal to conduct evaluations.

Question 7: What other
requirements am I likely to encounter?

There are a variety of requirements for teacher certification throughout the United States. Some states, and universities within the states, apply selected requirements to student teaching. For example, Alabama, Kentucky, Missouri, North Carolina, Texas, and Washington require minimum passing scores on a basic skills exam prior to student teaching. Several other states require a similar basic skills exam; however, the exam is a requirement for initial teacher certification only.

Other requirements for state certification that might be applied to student teaching may include a fee established by the university. For example, among Texas universities student teaching fees range from none to $250. Some states or school districts may require a clear TB test in order to student teach. Twelve states require coursework in special education prior to student teaching. Thirteen states require fingerprinting prior to obtaining initial teacher certification; states, universities, or school districts may require some form of criminal history check prior to admission to student teaching. More than half of the states require a screening of moral character for teacher certification; some universities may require a statement by professors, advisers, or department chairs that the student is morally fit to student teach.

When investigating requirements for student teaching in another state, it is advisable to inquire about state certification requirements. It is possible that a student could meet student teaching requirements at a particular university, yet not meet state certification requirements. The university certification officer is able to assist in this inquiry.

Summary

A student transferring to another state for student teaching might have questions other than those addressed above. As indicated earlier in this chapter, differing requirements and expectations are adhered to by individual states and universities. Therefore, students are encouraged to contact the director of student teaching or field experience at a particular university for detailed guidelines and requirements. Prior to the initial contact, the student is advised to develop a list of pertinent questions so that the director or adviser can adequately address specific needs and concerns.

Reference

Andrews, T. E., & Andrews, L. (Eds.). (1994). *The NASDTEC manual 1994-1995. National association of state directors of teacher education and certification*. Dubuque, IA: Kendall/Hunt.

Creating the
Student Teaching Handbook

GLORIA APPELT SLICK

The Importance of a
Well-Developed Student Teaching Handbook

In a previous chapter the issue of communication as a key factor in the success of field experience programs was mentioned. The major purpose of a field experience handbook or student teaching handbook is to communicate. Of all the written communication produced by the field experience office, this one document probably has more impact on public relations than any other. It holds the guiding principles of the whole field experience program and thereby represents a major portion of the university's teacher preparation program. Every effort should be made to produce a polished, professional document.

This chapter addresses the purposes and key components of the field experience handbook. Suggestions are included that concern the type of style and presentation format to use. It is quite possible to have a significant amount of information in a handbook that might or might not be readily accessible. Being able to find things easily becomes a prime consideration for the user. Most handbooks specifically address the student teaching experience and requirements for certification. Many times the handbook is the primary form of communication that explains the program to students, university personnel, and the public schools. Consequently, a well-organized, clearly written document is a high priority.

Once the document is printed and in the hands of the users, it is very important to take the time to provide the users with meetings that will present an overview of the contents and processes for accessing the information. This will also be an opportunity for the users to ask questions about the program. You can then refer them to the section(s) in the handbook that answer their questions.

Organization of the Student Teaching Handbook

After a review of more than 300 handbooks collected from field directors around the nation, some common characteristics of the more helpful ones emerged.

I. Introduction: Typically the beginning sections of the student teaching handbook will include the following:

A statement of the program's philosophy and/or mission

A professional code of ethics

Acknowledgments

Definitions of terms critical to the understanding of the concepts in the handbook; that is, student teacher, student teaching, cooperating teacher, university supervisor, cooperating school, and the like

Goals and objectives of the program: The goals are generally stated in terms of the program outcomes, but the objectives may be stated in terms of student outcomes

The following is a sample philosophy/mission statement taken from The University of Southern Mississippi's *Student Teaching Handbook—A Guide for Student Teachers, Supervising Teachers, and University Coordinators*:

> The Office of Educational Field Experiences seeks to provide experiences that allow our university students the transitional opportunity for practical application of knowledge base and pedagogical skills. These experiences include observation, assessment, planning, presentation and evaluation within the pre-service teaching experience. At all levels of field experiences, the university student should be developing a repertoire of professional skills and competencies that will prepare and continue to educate them to be outstanding professional educators. (Office of Educational Field Experiences, 1994, p. 1)

The introductory part of the handbook provides the philosophic base and often the knowledge base expectations for the program. Generally speaking, the remainder of the handbook explains who and how the people involved will accomplish the mission of the program.

II. Table of Contents: The table of contents is critical because it basically outlines the organizational format and content of the handbook. Careful consideration to the logical placement of the handbook components will assist users in finding the information pertinent to their needs. Some of the major sections to include in the handbook are (see also Figure 9.1 below):

> Roles and Responsibilities of Participants: description of the individual participant's roles and corresponding responsibilities
> Program Policies and Procedures: state and university requirements, and legal status of students while in the public schools

Assessment Policies and Procedures: explanation of the use of the various evaluation documents

Program Timeline/Schedule

Instruction and Planning Guidelines

Questions and Answers (includes questions and their answers to questions most frequently asked by students, university supervisors, and cooperating teachers)

Appendices: including sample copies of documents to be used in the program, that is, lesson plan form, evaluation forms, daily and/or weekly report forms, and the like

Because the handbook usually covers the field experience program thoroughly and often gives an overview of the entire teacher preparation program, it becomes a very important public relations tool. It is the document that is most frequently seen by public school personnel. Therefore, a well-organized, professionally formatted handbook can leave a lasting, positive impression about your university's teacher education program.

III. Organizational Options: There are some topics that need to be addressed in the field experience handbook that are general to all the persons involved in the various field experiences provided students. The topics listed below should probably each be in separate sections. Doing this will help the reader locate the information more easily.

General Topics:

A. *Program Policies and Procedures:* This section would include information that deals with university, state, and national requirements for program completion and certification.

1. Eligibility requirements for teacher education certification and specifically for student teaching
2. Student teaching placement procedures
3. Change in placement procedures

Table of Contents

Figure 9.1. Sample Table of Contents

    4. Legal status of student teachers in respective states

    5. Department of education teacher certification standards, both state and national

B. *Assessment Policies:* This section of the handbook would give definitive descriptions of the processes of evaluation that are a part of the program. It would specifically define each participant's responsibilities in the evaluation process. Since the overall grading process results in a common enterprise, it should therefore be included in a separate section addressing only evaluation procedures.

    1. Evaluation Guidelines—present the philosophy and explanations of the program grading policies.

    2. Evaluation of the student teacher

       a. University supervisor responsibilities—gathering of formative data through observations and checklists; using formative data and final evaluation assessment forms to write a narrative summary evaluation; qualitative assessment of the student's teaching portfolio; ongoing feedback conferences

       b. Cooperating teacher responsibilities—gather formative data through observations and checklists; making final summative evaluation using outcomes-based criteria; ongoing feedback conferences

       c. Student teacher self-evaluation responsibilities

          1) Reflective journal

          2) Audio- and/or videotaped lesson for self-analysis

          3) Development of a portfolio

       d. School administrator evaluation responsibilities

    3. Guidelines for determining the student teacher's final grade and an explanation of the grade marking system.

       For example:

          Excellent. An "A" indicates that the student performed at the highest level of proficiency and consistently took initiative above and beyond basic requirements.

Very Good. A "B" indicates that the student performed above average and met all program requirements to the best of his or her ability.

Adequate. A "C" indicates that the student satisfactorily completed all of the program requirements; however, he or she still needs improvement in some areas (Office of Educational Field Experiences, 1994, p. 70).

4. Copies of Assessment Forms—sample evaluation forms should be included so students, university supervisors, and cooperating teachers have a reference form with which to study and become familiar. Any instrument or data collection form used by any one of the principal evaluators, including the self-assessment instruments, should be included.

C. *Program Timelines:* Included in this section should be:

1. Calendar dates for the beginning, middle, and ending of the student teaching experiences
2. Scheduled seminar meeting dates and topics
3. Suggested weekly schedule of events and responsibilities for the student teacher, cooperating teacher, and university supervisor
4. Schedule of due dates for forms and reports that are due to the field experience office
5. A graphic depiction of the phase-in and phase-out timeline of the responsibilities of the student teacher and cooperating teacher during student teaching
6. A narrative description, in brief summary form, corresponding to a timeline of the phase-in and phase-out responsibilities of the student teacher and cooperating teacher (see Figure 9.2)

D. *Question and Answer Section:* This section should include the questions most frequently asked by student teachers, cooperating teachers, and university supervisors. Most of the questions will be of interest and assistance to all three major participants. For exam-

Suggested Schedule for Student Teaching

Week	Student Teacher	Cooperating Teacher	University Supervisor
1	observe in classroom	discuss plans and activities with student	initial visit: dissemination of forms, discussion of handbook, requirements, and expectations
	orientation to school, school policies, and students	provide ample opportunities for observation	
	work with individual students	provide opportunity for review of school policies and procedures	
	after 3 to 5 days, teach at least 1 lesson*	provide opportunity for review of pupil records	
	evaluate daily activities		
	daily conference with cooperating teacher about the day's activities and lessons	conference with university supervisor	
		complete required university forms	
	begin daily reflective journals	familiarize yourself with the student teacher's biographical information	
	complete university forms		

* First lessons taught may be prepared by supervising teacher.

(Continued)

Figure 9.2. Sample Phase-In and Phase-Out Timeline

ple, the following question is typically asked by the school administrator as well: May the student teacher substitute teach? (Note: Answers will be specific to individual program policies and state regulations.)

Week	Student Teacher	Cooperating Teacher	University Supervisor
2	continue observing in classroom	allow student to teach additional lessons*	initial visit may overlap into 2nd week
	begin to assume more teaching responsibility	review student's work on instructional unit portfolio	
	begin working on instructional unit portfolio		
		allow for continued observation	
	observe in other classrooms	complete university forms	
	continue daily discussions with cooperating teacher		
	evaluate daily activities		
	continue daily reflective journal entries		
	complete university forms		

Figure 9.2. Continued

E. *Appendices:* The appendices may contain sample forms of data collection documents, program correspondence, lesson plan format, and the student teaching application. Sometimes the documents included in the appendices are extensions of guidelines presented in the regular text. Other times they may be handouts that provide helpful information on such topics as motivation, classroom management, how to establish rapport with your cooperating teacher and pupils in your class, and other helpful information.

Week	Student Teacher	Cooperating Teacher	University Supervisor
3	assume more teaching responsibility: prepare lesson plans, teach additional periods	allow student to assume greater teaching responsibility in the classroom	conduct practice observation evaluation
			hold conference with teacher and student
	teach class for practice observation evaluation; cooperating teacher and university supervisor provide feedback	review student's draft of instructional unit portfolio	
		complete university forms as required	
	submit draft of instructional unit portfolio for review by cooperating teacher and university supervisor	conduct practice teaching evaluation	
	observe in other classrooms		
	evaluate daily activities		
	continue daily reflective journal entries		*(Continued)*

A student teacher is responsible for a minimum of 2 weeks up to a maximum of 3 weeks of full-time teaching responsibilities (minimum of 4 instructional periods).

Figure 9.2. Continued

Specific Topics:

These topics should receive special attention and probably will merit an individual section in the handbook. As mentioned

Week	Student Teacher	Cooperating Teacher	University Supervisor
5-6	submit instructional unit portfolio for evaluation by university supervisor and cooperating teacher	evaluate student portfolio	evaluate student portfolio and conduct conference with teacher and student teacher
	assume total teaching responsibility in classroom	allow student to take complete teaching responsibility with the class, providing support as needed	conduct final classroom observation depending upon schedule
	suspend out-of-classroom observations	complete university forms as required	conduct follow-up conference subsequent to final classroom observation (PS/IS)
	evaluate daily activities	conduct final classroom observation depending upon schedule	
	be prepared for final classroom observation depending on unit schedule		
	continue daily reflective journal entries		

Figure 9.2. Continued

earlier, the roles and responsibilities of the major publics involved in the field experience program may be handled separately, to specifically address the persons and/or responsibilities being presented. For example, many handbooks address the roles and responsibilities of the student teacher, university personnel, and public school personnel in a special section of the handbook. Regardless of whether the roles and responsibilities of the key people in the supervision paradigm are handled in one section or in separate ones, the following topics should be covered:

Week	Student Teacher	Cooperating Teacher	University Supervisor
7-8	gradually decrease teaching responsibilities	conference with university supervisor	receive and grade notebooks
	continue observing in other classrooms	gradually resume teaching responsibility	conduct final seminar/close out conference with student teacher
	return all materials borrowed from cooperating teacher and school	complete university forms	
	submit self-evaluation to university supervisor		

Figure 9.2. Continued

A. *Student Teachers:* preservice teachers engaged in full-time public school placements for the purpose of applying teaching skills and knowledge in the classroom setting. The section of the handbook that addresses issues related to the student teacher should include:

1. A set of goals for which the student teacher should strive
2. Specific program requirements for which the student teacher is responsible
3. Explanations of various assignments associated with the student teaching program:
   a. Reflective processes—journals, critiques, and so on
   b. Uses of multimedia, computers, bulletin boards
   c. Observations and critiques
   d. Unit and lesson plan guidelines
   e. Portfolio development

4. Program policies
    a. Attendance requirements
    b. Code of ethics:
        1) Confidentiality
        2) Professional demeanor
        3) Professional dress
        4) Respect toward pupils, all professionals, and parents
5. Student teaching seminars
6. Relationships with cooperating teacher and university supervisor
7. Legal status of student teachers during student teaching
8. Student teacher professional responsibilities
9. Reports and record-keeping responsibilities:
    a. Student teacher progress report
    b. Weekly schedule report
    c. Daily journal entries
    d. Self-evaluation checklist
    e. Audio- or videotaped teaching of a lesson
10. Special information to help the student teacher
    a. Classroom management guidelines
    b. Motivation procedures
    c. Learning styles information
    d. Sample lesson plans

B. *Public School Personnel:*

Cooperating Teachers: The public school field teacher who guides and nurtures the preservice teacher. This person serves as a role model and mentor for the neophyte teacher. He or she shares the classroom, students, expertise, and advice with the student teacher. The special section set aside for the cooperating teacher should provide information about:

1. How to prepare for a student teacher (see Figure 9.3)

2. How to prepare pupils for the student teacher
3. How to conduct constructive conferences
4. Methods for providing effective feedback
5. Guidelines for planning with the student teacher
6. Guidelines for collaborative teaching
7. How to be an effective evaluator and mentor for the student teacher
8. How to be an effective observer and reporter of observations
9. Expectations in terms of program requirements
10. General guidelines for effective supervision
11. Eligibility requirements to be a cooperating teacher (particular to state and university requirements)
12. Rewards and recognition bestowed upon cooperating teachers by the university and/or the LEA

The Cooperating District and School: The handbook should provide a description of the role and responsibilities of the central office personnel and campus site administrator(s) with regard to the placement of university students in the district.

Information in this section should include:

1. University-district contract status
2. Program placement policies and procedures
3. Role and responsibilities of the central office contact person
4. Role and responsibilities of the building principal, for example:
   a. Soliciting qualified volunteer teachers for student teachers
   b. Preparing cooperating teachers for the student teacher
   c. Welcoming student teachers, orienting to school and program
   d. Observation and evaluation responsibilities
   e. Serve as an instructional model and professional resource

1. Prepare the pupils for a student teacher's arrival.

    ___Inform pupils of the impending arrival.

    ___Tell pupils something about the student teacher.

    ___Create a feeling of anticipation for a student teacher's arrival.

    ___Other

2. Learn about the student teacher's background.

    ___Subject knowledge

    ___Pre-student teaching field experiences

    ___Special interests or skills

    ___Other

3. Read the college student teaching handbook.

    ___Understand basic responsibilities.

    ___Review requirements and expectations for cooperating teachers.

    ___Other

4. Become aware of the legal status of student teachers.

    ___Responsibility of supervising teacher when a student teacher covers a class

    ___Other

5. Become familiar with school policy concerning student teacher responsibilities.

    ___Reporting to school

    ___Absences

    ___Attendance at faculty meetings

    ___Supervisory activities

    ___Other

6. Make a pre-teaching contact with the student teacher.

    ___Letter of introduction

    ___Student introduction

    ___Encourage a pre-teaching visit

    ___Other

Figure 9.3. Supervising Teacher's Checklist for a Student Teacher's Arrival

7. Secure copies of materials to be used in orienting student teacher.

___School handbook

___Daily schedule

___Seating charts

___Other

8. Make necessary arrangements for the student teacher to be comfortable in the classroom.

___Arrange for a desk or table

___Have necessary supplies

___Prepare a file of necessary and informative materials

___Other

9. Secure copies of teaching resources for the student teacher.

___Textbooks

___Curriculum guides

___Resource books

___Other

10. Develop a plan for the student teacher's entry into teaching.

___Introduction to the class

___Introduction to the faculty

___Initial teaching activities

___Other

Planning Notes:

Figure 9.3. Continued

    f. Provide opportunities for student teachers to shadow the principal to learn about the life of an administrator

University Personnel: In this section of the handbook, descriptions of the roles and responsibilities of the people operating the field experience office as well as those persons supervising in the field should be provided. The persons whose jobs need to be described are:

1. The director of field experiences
2. The assistant director
3. The administrative assistant/executive secretary
4. The secretary/clerk
5. The university supervisors

Other special sections that might be included in a field experiences handbook would be:

A. *Preparing for the Job*

1. Interview guidelines
2. Application processes
3. Proper telephone etiquette
4. Professional dress and comportment

B. *Departmental Section:* In this section of the handbook, information specific to the various departments in which teacher preparation programs reside may need to be shared. Content area and specialty area expectations can be described that will provide students and cooperating teachers with more specific guidelines for respective certification areas.

C. *Follow-Up Evaluation:* This special section should include an evaluation document that can be used to determine the field experience program's success in terms of student satisfaction. There should be two documents with different dimensions of response. One should be an immediate feedback evaluation completed at the end of the student teaching experience. The other should be an evaluation form completed and sent back to the university at the end of the student's first-year teaching experience. The students should report at that time how they feel about the teacher preparation program they experienced, in particular the field experiences component, after they have taught for 1 year.

Not only will this information aid the university faculty as they plan their instructional and experiential agendas, but it will also work toward satisfying NCATE's (National Council for the Accreditation of Teacher Education) concern about follow-up connections with our programs' graduates. Provide the forms, which can be easily removed from the handbook, and self-addressed, postage-paid envelopes so that the students can readily return the evaluation surveys.

Field Experience Handbook Formats

Up to this point, this chapter has focused on the contents of a well-organized and informative handbook. That the contents of the handbook are critical to the overall program goes without saying. Equally important, but for different yet connected reasons, is the format of the handbook. As decisions are made regarding the handbook format, one must remember the various publics for which the document is intended. Also, it is important to bear in mind, above all else, the issue of making the document and the information in it physically easy to read and readily accessible. The following are important considerations to make with regard to format:

A. *Size:* Most handbooks are printed on letter-size paper; therefore, they conform to most materials commonly carried and stored by persons in the profession. A few are approximately the size of 5×7 index cards. They resemble small organizational directories.

B. *Opening Orientation:* It is important to decide the direction of the handbook opening: Will the book be opened in the traditional left-to-right manner, or perhaps from top to bottom? Most handbooks follow the traditional left-to-right opening process.

C. *Binding:* There are several options for binding a handbook. Many questions need to be answered when determining the binding process to be used on the handbook, not the least of which is cost. The options include (a) stapling—least expensive, but difficult to do if the document is very thick; (b) gluing—fairly expensive and requires both special formatting of pages and print shop expertise; (c) stitching—very expensive and also requires special page formatting and print shop expertise; (d) plastic comb, hole-punched and assembled—requires a special machine to assemble, but the spiral-type feature of this option allows for easy page turning of the document; and (e) hole-punching for a three-ring binder—one of the least expensive ways and probably the most flexible way to bind the document. Judging from the 300 documents surveyed, the most popular means of binding is stapling. The next most frequently used binding is the plastic comb. The most recent handbook created for The University of Southern Mississippi was designed for a three-ring binder. The handbook contents were created on the Macintosh LC, 7.0, which provided a laser-print copy of the entire document, including the document cover sheets. This laser-print copy was sent to the print shop for duplication of 500 copies. The print shop duplicated the document and three-hole punched it for an approximate cost of $3 per document copy. The contents were shrink-wrapped to create a package for students to purchase at the bookstore. The students are then able to choose the type of three-ring binder that they prefer for storing the handbook contents. Students have reported their pleasure in working with this particular format because it allows them more flexibility in both adding information and accessing the information in the document. An additional feature that has made the document a success are the tabbed section dividers that identify each section in the handbook. These tabs are easily read and clearly mark topical sections in the handbook. From the field experience office perspective, the three-ring binder style is highly advantageous because it provides an easy way to add or delete material without having to reprint and rebind the entire document. With so many changes occurring in the profession at the state and national levels, flexibility in changing the information needed and provided in the handbook is a welcome relief. Cooperating teachers have also indicated that they like the new format because of the ease in turning pages and finding information. For each type of format, there are pros and cons for selecting one over the others. The main criterion, I believe, is making the document relevant and usable.

D. Type of Paper: The weight of the paper is indicative of the quality of the document in terms of its lasting ability, as well as perhaps the quality of the program. Although most of us are operating on limited budgets, please recall the important point made earlier in this chapter: *The field experiences handbook is an important public relations tool.* Providing a quality document that explains a very critical component of our teacher preparation programs sends a strong message to our field partners and the community in general. In addition to the actual contents, the type, color, and weight of the paper used are going to have an impact on the quality of the final product. Regular 20- to 30-pound quality can be used for the bulk of the document; however, the front, back, and dividers, if you have any in your book, should minimally be of card stock weight. Card stock comes in a variety of finishes: rough, smooth, dull, shiny.

E. Color: Color selection involves several decisions. Most handbooks are printed with black ink on white paper. However, the document cover, which is typically card stock quality, is often a contrasting color. Many times color selection is based on the university's varsity colors. This works fine unless the school colors are infrequently used ones (by printers), which make them more expensive. Black is the least expensive color to use for the ink/print color of the document manuscript. Dark blue or navy is the next least expensive. The prices begin to escalate when such colors as red, green, maroon, and the like are used.

F. Graphics: Graphics add a nice touch to any document. Three criteria for using them should be: (a) Can they be reproduced in a cost-effective manner? (b) Can they be created with an available computer program? and (c) Do they add a necessary dimension to the text that is critical to the conceptualization of the material in the document? Sometimes graphics are used for associative purposes, especially when they are the symbols of the university.

G. Print Style: The font (typeface) and point size used for the handbook manuscript are also important considerations. Some fonts are difficult to read but look pretty. Others are easy to read but are dull and unappealing to the eye. Finding a happy medium that looks professional, is easy to read, and has eye appeal is the key. Minimal point size should be 12-point, to make it easily read.

Conclusion

If you are a director of field experience programs and you are reading this chapter, you should have the distinct impression that one of your most important responsibilities is to create a very polished, informative, and professional handbook. This document represents what your office is all about and it reflects how important you feel your business is. Field directors have a wonderful opportunity to present themselves in a very organized and professional manner through a well-thought-out document that demonstrates to the world, among other things, just how complex and important our responsibilities are in the scheme of teacher preparation. I have tried to describe in detail the various topics that should be included in your handbook as well as specific guidelines to make decisions about the format of your document. I wish I could have had this information to guide my first attempts at producing this all-important document. Five years later, I have learned a lot, and I hope it will be beneficial to you.

Reference

Office of Educational Field Experiences. (1994). *Student teaching handbook—A guide for student teachers, supervising teachers, and university coordinators.* Hattiesburg: The University of Southern Mississippi.

Recommended Reading

Student Teaching and Field Experiences. (1990). *Handbook for student teaching.* Fort Wayne: School of Education, Indiana University/Purdue University.

❖ 10 ❖

Bits and Pieces

Everything Else You Wanted to Know About Operating Field Experience Programs

KENNETH BURRETT
GLORIA APPELT SLICK

What do we know about field experience programs and the people who run them? The programs include a mix of students, education faculty, and school district teachers and administrators. Teacher education students participate from their birth as declared majors until either graduation or termination. The field experience office operates 12 months a year, and often more than 8 hours a day. The field director's job definition is clear in regard to matching students with assigned places, posting lists, completing paperwork, hiring supervisors, and balancing budgets. Less clear are the tasks focusing on program leadership, establishing collaborative arrangements, influencing teacher education faculty, and impacting the philosophical and spiritual elements of teacher education programming.

The field director is an excellent manager of detail, of written communication, of office personnel, and of all items relating to operational efficiency. Often, the field office becomes the resource center for interpreting state certification regulations. Certainly, the image of the university is carried to the local education community through correspondence regarding field programming. Because those working in field experience offices always have more work and deadlines than time, more anxious students than counseling ability, and more return calls to make than phones to use, the field director is a compassionate and efficient taskmaster.

Successful programs are more than well run. Although single details receive attention, the total effectiveness depends upon the quality of the overall schema. The impact is achieved through the interrelations of the parts. In addition to a skill for managing individual tasks, running a successful program requires a penchant for the analytic, the creative, the innovative, and the transcendent mind.

So, you think you want to be a field director. Are you sure you are ready? Stop before you leap, and consider what you are about to do. Do you like people a lot? Do you like helping people work together compatibly? Are you familiar with the bureaucracy of both institutions of higher learning and public schools? Are you an expert public relations person? Do you like to work long hours and counsel everyone from colleagues to students' parents? Are you an effective arbiter? Do you work as a positive leader, using the participatory style of leadership? Are you comfortable in the public school setting? Are you familiar with contemporary state and national legislation that affect teacher education? These and many more questions should be going through your head as you consider taking on the responsibilities of a field director. The following is offered as a checklist of items to consider regarding the role and responsibilities of a field director. Review it carefully and assess your capabilities as a potential candidate for field director, or analyze your competencies as an acting director.

Category 1: People Skills. Field directors must be people who enjoy and appreciate people. They need to be people who appreciate diversity in others and know how to make the most of all that each individual can contribute. Consider the following and see if it describes you.

Field directors are people who:

1. Like people.
2. Enjoy and appreciate everyone's unique contribution to the total program.
3. Understand the need people have to feel wanted and appreciated.
4. Easily join work and task groups.
5. Invite others to feel comfortable in joining team groups.
6. Seek ways to make it possible for everyone to feel successful.
7. Know how to make people feel a part of the total effort.
8. Practice effective oral communication.
9. Motivate individuals and groups.

Category 2: Communication Skills. Field directors need to possess effective written and oral communication skills. The position of field director involves numerous times when written correspondence is the primary way that information is disseminated to contact persons in the public schools and across the university. The field director will have many opportunities to address interested persons, both formally and informally, and will therefore need to be comfortable conversing with large groups and one-on-one. Phone etiquette and clear use of language during a telephone conversation are also important. From time to time a director will find himself or herself handling a delicate placement situation over the phone. Choice of words and tone of voice can be very critical under these circumstances. Good relationships can be established or hindered by the way a phone call is handled. Check yourself on the following.

I am a person who can:

1. Construct a clear, concise, to-the-point memo.
2. Compose an effective letter that is friendly as well as informative.
3. Speak to large groups and successfully communicate ideas and processes.
4. Counsel students and help them make personal decisions for their benefit.
5. Engage in conversation with teachers and be received as an empathetic and credible listener.
6. Be perceived as knowledgeable about public schools and able to discuss issues pertinent to public school personnel.
7. Design and write program policies and procedures.
8. Design and write program handbooks.
9. Make large-group presentations via videotape and/or public television.
10. Communicate and negotiate well over the telephone or other media.

Category 3: Leadership and Management Skills. A field director is the kind of leader who must serve many publics and must constantly bring all those publics together in mind and deed for the benefit of all concerned. This requires the director to employ, under most conditions, a transformational type of leadership. There are times, however, when a field director must act in a more direct decision-making mode. The bottom line is that a field director must be able to adeptly apply the appropriate type of leadership style that matches the demands of the current situation in which he or she is operating. Consider the following when determining your qualifications for becoming a field director.

The field director leads by:

1. Providing all persons concerned the opportunity to contribute expertise to situations under discussion or to processes undergoing change.

2. Choosing leadership strategies that accurately fit the situation.

3. Effectively reflecting on past events and making appropriate adjustments accordingly.

4. Carefully selecting personnel who can work cooperatively with others in a team mode.

5. Creating representative committees whose purpose is to give advice about program operation and changes.

6. Initiating ongoing evaluation of the program's operation and effectiveness.

7. Modeling effective collaboration strategies for university as well as public school personnel.

8. Engaging in research that considers state-of-the-art possibilities for program advancement and/or improvement.

9. Establishing operational procedures for smooth office management.

10. Creating, with the assistance of the office staff, a year-round schedule of events and tasks to be accomplished in order for the office to run efficiently.

11. Providing all personnel clear and cooperatively determined expectations of the roles and responsibilities of their jobs.

Category 4: Background Experience and the Knowledge Base. Field directors live in the university community and the world of elementary and secondary schools. As such, there is a need to have total empathy with the pressures and priorities that come with immersion in schools and children's classrooms. Field programs prepare teacher education candidates to function in the schools of today, yet one of the goals of teacher education is to prepare teachers for the schools of tomorrow, the 21st century. The director will be a source of practical and pragmatic advice, supporting the process of socializing the teacher education students into the schools of today. At other occasions, the director will support students and encourage school teachers to engage in cutting-edge practices in the classroom and support new paradigms for school practice. The field director is both a sage and a prophet.

A field director is an educational expert who:

1. Possesses insight into the daily working of elementary and secondary schooling, usually gained through experience and study.
2. Works comfortably within the administrative structure of contemporary elementary and secondary schools.
3. Understands the theoretical underpinnings of school organization.
4. Is conversant with theories of classroom management and instruction.
5. Understands leadership theory.
6. Can support change as well as the status quo.
7. Works constructively with university faculty in program development.
8. Understands school structure and restructuring.
9. Is committed to excellence in practice.
10. Can relate academic knowledge, vision, and action.

Postscript

Have you answered the questions? Did you complete the checklists? Are you ready, willing, and able to assume the challenge? Know yourself and understand the position. Here is an opportunity to organize, manage, influence, and lead. Nowhere else is it possible to have a greater impact on the next generation of teachers. There is no better opportunity to connect the world of theory with the world of practice. The position of director of field experience is for those who are committed to program excellence, can share in the joys and tribulations involved in the quest for teaching excellence, and can manage today to dream of tomorrow.

Index

CORWIN
PRESS

The Corwin Press Logo—a raven striding across an open book—represents the happy union of courage and learning. We are a professional-level publisher of books and journals for K-12 educators, and we are committed to creating and providing resources that embody these qualities. Corwin's motto is "Success for All Learners."